The Authorities

~ Powerful Wisdom from Leaders in the Field ~

ANDRE DAWKINS

Mortgage Broker

AuthoritiesPress

Copyright © 2018 Authorities Press

ISBN: 978-1-77277-231-9

Publisher
Authorities Press
Markham, ON
Canada

Printed in the United States and Canada.

TESTIMONIALS

"Dear Andre, Just want to say a very BIG THANK YOU! You truly go the extra distance for your customers, keep up the great work! You will definitely continue to be successful." – God bless you!, Angela Stewart

"Dear Andre, I contacted Andre at Expert Mortgage and was relieved when he provided me with several workable options for self-employed individuals like myself. Because my business was fairly new, it was very difficult for me to get a standard mortgage and none of banks would approve my applications. When I called Andre (late in the night) and explained my circumstances to him, he went to work right away and within a couple of days provided me with a great solution that allowed me to get a mortgage with a mainstream lender at a very competitive rate. Because of my schedule, Andre was flexible and worked with me after hours to finalize the deal. He was prompt, knowledgably, professional and honest. I would definitely recommend him if you are in a situation where the regular channels are not an option for you. Great service." – K I

"Dear Andre, We wanted to take this opportunity to thank you for all you have done for us during the last month since meeting you. We believe that without your help it wouldn't have been possible to have this new financial reality and stability available to us. You were also very professional, patient and extremely knowledgeable in every aspect of our financial needs as a growing family ... we couldn't have hoped to meet a better expert to take on the challenge of helping with our situation. Thank you sincerely and we look forward to doing business with you in the future!" – S & M

FOREWORD

Experts are to be admired for their knowledge, but they often remain unrecognized by the general public because they save their information and insights for paying customers and clients. There are many experts in a given field, but their impact is limited to the handful of people with whom they work.

Unlike experts, authorities share their knowledge and expertise far more broadly, so they make a big impact on the world. Authorities become known and admired as leading experts and, as such, typically do very well economically and professionally. Most authorities are also mature enough to know that part of the joy of monetary success is the accompanying moral and spiritual obligation to give back.

Many people want to learn and work with well-respected and generous authorities, but don't always know where to find them. They may be known to their peers, or within a specific community, but have not had the opportunity to reach a wider audience. At one time, they might have submitted a proposal to the For Dummies or Chicken Soup for the Soul series of books, but it's now almost impossible to get accepted as a new author in such branded book series.

It is more than fitting that Raymond Aaron, an internationally known and respected authority in his own right, would be the one to recognize the need for a new venue in which authorities could share their considerable knowledge with readers everywhere. As the only author ever to be included in both of the book series mentioned above, Raymond has had the opportunity to give back and he understands how crucial it is for authorities to have a platform from which to share their expertise.

I have known and worked with Raymond for a number of years and consider him a valued friend and talented coach. He knows how to spot talented and knowledgeable people and he desires to see them prosper. Over the years, success coaching and speaking engagements around the world have made it possible for Raymond to meet many of these talented authorities. He recognizes and relates to their passion and enthusiasm for what they do, as well as their desire to share what they know. He tells me that's why he created this new nonfiction branded book series, The Authorities.

Dr. Nido Qubein
President, High Point University

TABLE OF CONTENTS

INTRODUCTION

This book introduces you to *The Authorities* — individuals who have distinguished themselves in life and in business. Authorities make a big impact on the world. Authorities are leaders in their chosen fields. Authorities typically do very well financially, and are evolved enough to know that part of the joy of monetary success is the accompanying social, moral and spiritual obligation to give back.

Authorities are not just outstanding. They are also *known* to be outstanding.

This additional element begins to explain the difference between two strategic business and life concepts — one that seems great, but isn't, and the other that fills in the essential missing gap of the first.

The first concept is "the expert."

What is an expert? The real definition is ...

EXPERT: *a person who knows stuff*

People who have attained a very senior academic degree (like a PhD or an MD) definitely know stuff. People who read voraciously and retain what they read definitely know stuff. Unfortunately, just because you know stuff does not mean that anyone respects the fact that you do. Even though some experts are successful, alas, most are not — because knowing stuff is not enough.

Well, then, what is the missing piece?

What the expert lacks, "the authority" has. The authority both knows stuff and is *known* to know stuff. So, more simply ...

AUTHORITY: *a person who is known as an expert*

The difference is not subtle. The difference is not merely semantic. The difference is enormous.

When it comes to this subject, there are actually three categories in which people fall:

- People who don't know much and are unsuccessful in life and in business. Most people fall in this category.

- People who know stuff, but still don't leave much of a footprint in the world. There are a lot of people like this.

- Experts who are also *known* as experts become authorities and authorities are always wondrously successful. Authorities are able to contribute more to humanity through both their chosen work and their giving back.

This book is about the highest category, *The Authorities* — people who have reached the peak in their field and are known as such.

You will definitely know some of *The Authorities* in this book, especially since there are some world-famous ones. Others are just as exceptional, but you may not yet know about them. Our featured author, Andre Dawkins, is the upcoming author of the book Mortgages on Fire. Andre has two passions: music and helping people. On the work side of things, he is living the dream, passionately helping people to get financing for all their real estate needs. He has been in the mortgage industry for 10 years. When Andre first started, it was difficult to find a way to allow people to trust him to work on the most important investment of their lives. He found it frustrating, however, he kept on pounding the pavement to make sure he would come out on top.

Andre is the youngest of five siblings. Being the youngest allowed him to watch and see what he could and should do … and what he shouldn't do. He was able to stay ahead of the curve by having older siblings clear the path for him. Born in Toronto but raised in Brampton, Ontario in Canada from an early age, he learned the life lesson that hard work always pays off.

At 16, Andre began working two jobs and, technically, continued working two or more jobs for all his life until the end of 2015, when he made a stand and decided to do mortgages full time. He has not looked back since. He has always been a go-getter and a visionary. Andre can recall when he was 15 and would tell his friends that he was going to get his license next year at 16, and they would say, "For what, so you can drive your parent's car?" he told them to watch and they would see ...

Then lo and behold at 16, with working two jobs, from his humble beginnings at Red Lobster as a dishwasher and at Winners Warehouse doing general labour, he was able to save up for his first car. Wow, what an accomplishment! Andre now knew there was nothing that he put his mind to that he couldn't achieve.

Throughout Andre's career he has worked in many capacities that has helped to build him into a great mortgage broker. Perhaps the greatest of these was the development of his brand. So, please remember that when you need a mortgage: CALL ANDRE at 1.647.991.7325

They are *The Authorities*. Learn from them. Connect with them. Let them uplift you. Learning from them and working with them is the secret ingredient for success which may well allow you to rise to the level of Authority soon.

To be considered for inclusion in a subsequent edition of *The Authorities*, register to attend a future event at www.aaron.com/events where you will be interviewed and considered.

Branding Into Greatness

ANDRE DAWKINS

We all have greatness within us. The deciding factor is our will. Nothing that happens in life has any meaning unless we CHOOSE to make it so. Are you used to making quick decisions, or do you tend to procrastinate? Do you have strong will power? Do you act on emotion or on the thoughts you consciously choose? The answers to questions like these matter a great deal when it comes to greatness. Do you choose meanings consciously? Do you choose meanings that work for you instead of against you? Or do you react to situations based on emotion? Whatever you do, remember that you always achieve when you choose to put all your might into doing something good.

1

I'm a mortgage broker. A great one. It's why, if you're looking into investing in real estate, you should **CALL ANDRE at 1.647.991.7325**. Consider the following …

- Instead of going to a bank for a home loan you can have me work on your behalf to both shop your rate with multiple lenders and manage your loan application from start to finish.
- Often times, when going to a bank directly to apply for a loan, you could instantly jeopardize your chance of approval by simply saying the wrong thing
- I can shop your rate for you at various banks. For example: Bank A may have the lowest mortgage rate available, Bank B may have the lowest closing costs available and Bank C may have the best combination of rate and fees.
- I'm your loan guide and can be very accessible and hands-on from start to finish, and I may find a home for your loan among my many lending partners, which is especially useful if you've been denied elsewhere. I can also provide more advanced/tailored recommendations or structure your loan favorably to lower costs.
- When it comes to your credit, I specialize in credit building and repairing, so I can provide you with a blueprint to get your credit on par.
- I can offer all types of home loans, from conventional options to non-conforming stuff. I typically offer a wide product choice because of my many partners.
- NOTE: like all other loan originators, I charge fees for my services. Additionally, I may get compensated from the lender I connect you with. But remember that I can offer competitive rates that meet or beat those of retail banks, so I should be considered alongside banks

when searching for financing. Typically, if you qualify at the bank and I arrange your mortgage, there will be no fees. I also have the ability to shop numerous lenders at once so I can find the best pricing based on your needs.

If the Bank says No ... **CALL ANDRE at 1.647.991.7325**

So the bank turns you down. This may seem like the end of the world, but it's not. There are many lenders out there, and I know a lot of them. Chances are with me to walk you through every step of the mortgage process, you'll find a home for your loan with one of my many partners. Here are some things you should know:

- All banks are not created equal. For example, every lender uses different policies and criteria when assessing your application— even if they're from the same parent company. I have access to this information and can match you up with a lender whose policies best suit your circumstances. To do this yourself, you'd have to go to each lender individually and assess their loan criteria and policies. Using me allows you to avoid this hassle and target the bank best suited to you.
- When you apply for a loan, it's crucial to realize that it will be registered on your credit file. This means you really don't want to shop around. You see, enquiries happen each time you apply for any kind of finance or credit (even entering a mobile phone contract) and can affect your ability to obtain credit in the future. Applying for loan after loan will actively destroy the likelihood that you'll ever be approved-- due to the number of enquiries building up on your credit file!
- Lenders don't like serial applicants, so rather than tackling a new loan application on your own, let me match you up with a suitable product

first time around, to avoid this trap.

- Getting your ducks in a row. I'll be able to tell you what you can do to improve your chances of being approved for a loan—for example, waiting until you've been at your job a few more months before you apply, or closing the credit card with the large limit that's reducing your borrowing power.

- I'm also an expert in low-doc loans, perfect for those who are self-employed or have a hazy credit history. I'll even tell you exactly what paperwork is required, and how to get around any obstacles in the criteria set by different lenders.

- It's to my advantage to get you the best possible deal, as I want to maintain positive relationships with my lenders, thereby knowing I will never put you into a product you can't afford. My intention is to have nothing but happy clients that have only great things to say about the service they received from my team and myself, so they can refer their friends and family to have the same experience.

I'll also be hoping you give me a good review, as I build my business partly from referrals—so it's always in my best interest to do the best thing by you.

By working with me, you could secure yourself a loan with a much lower interest rate or bonus features, potentially saving you tens of thousands of dollars over the life of the loan. Whether you're an investor or a homebuyer, if you would like further information and guidance about securing finance after your bank has said no, **CALL ANDRE at 1.647.991.7325**.

WHY YOU NEED A MORTGAGE BROKER

- They're mortgage experts who provide different lenders, loan types and rates for buyers without upfront charges.

- They can offer loan and rate options that a traditional bank may not be able to.
- They gather and manage critical paperwork while coordinating loan information with relevant parties.
- They help create your loan and close your home buying transaction properly.
- They typically close on your home faster than a traditional bank.
- You're not locked into working with a mortgage broker, and if for any reason they're not providing exceptional service, you can change brokers.

MARKET AWARENESS ... IN TERMS OF HOW BRANDING HAS ALLOWED ME TO STAND OUT IN THE MARKETPLACE.

When I first started doing mortgages, it was a constant struggle. It felt like everywhere I would turn there was doubt and closed doors. It felt as if I would never see success in this industry at all.

I keep telling myself, there has got to be a way, I gave my all to carve a niche into the marketplace. It all spiralled from the moment I adopted the principle slogan "if the bank says NO WAY? Better Call Andre!" It felt as if immediately a lightbulb went off in the consumers' eyes. Now, I'm not saying that all of a sudden everyone came running to me, however, the point is with the brand evolution it created an arena for me to play in. Once I came to the realization that I had something positive here, I immediately began my quest to build brand awareness through marketing.

I first started doing door to door hand outs of flyers that I would bring to a selected area. I was on a shoestring budget and had to make it because my "Y or why" was bigger than my how. I didn't know how it was going to happen, but I knew why it needed to happen. I was fed up with mediocrity, so I began visualizing myself as being successful. I began envision the life I wanted to create through the funnelling of my mortgage business. Then I applied my foot on the gas and keep it moving. Fast forward, I am constantly working on building and evolving my brand awareness. I was once told, closed mouths don't get fed. That hit home, as I came to realize the more the market knows of your existence, then the more the market can come to you for support and service.

I stand on the principles that I am here to serve, care for and change the lives of all my clients and customers—one deal at a time.

The moment I started making sales, I reinvested into marketing. I was fortunate to be working a full time job and earning a handsome salary. Therefore, all the mortgage money I made went right into advertising. I first put an ad in a local newspaper called SHARE newspaper, then later I put an ad on a local radio station G98.7 FM. To date, I still advertise in those two mediums because it was that foundation which allowed me to have such great market penetration.

The best part is I am only warming up. I plan to become a household name where "Call Andre" becomes a brand that is well recognized by the public.

Be on the lookout for the CA Mortgage Group: we will be expanding the brand into a more user-friendly platform from a standpoint of other agents using the Call Andre systems and techniques to serve, care for and change the lives of their customers. This is so they don't have to say I'm a mortgage agent/broker at the Call Andre Mortgage Group. The sound of CA Mortgage Group will be more appealing. But don't get confused: Call Andre is here to stay. The brand, the focus, the mission, the greatness … We are here to serve.

THINGS THE BANK WON'T TELL YOU

- You don't need a high credit score to qualify for a loan. If you're under the impression that you need a 720 credit score or higher to score the home of your dreams, think again. Many mortgage lenders require a minimum score of 680 to secure a loan. If you are applying for a High Ratio (insured mortgage with less than 20% down) mortgage loan, you may even qualify with a score of 600.

- Banks claim to have the best interest rates and have your best interest at heart, so how come it is that if you go to your bank to get a mortgage, they quote you a rate? They don't give you the best rate from the beginning. Why is it that you have to then re-approach them with a competitor rate to get them to match it.

- They usually have hidden clauses in their products that they do not inform you of. For example, a collateral charge ... where they register a higher amount on the title than the actual mortgage you are getting. In other words, they hold your equity hostage.

- The penalties to break your mortgage with a big bank are a lot higher than some of the same "A" lending institutions that mortgage brokers can get you into, and they are federally regulated just like a bank. They are called monoline lenders; monoline because they only have one line of business and that, of course, is mortgages. So they will not try to cross sell you and ultimately try to sink you in more debt.

- Fees and rates vary between lenders. Don't be afraid to shop around a little bit before deciding on a mortgage lender. Typically, each lender charges different origination fees and closing costs. While it may only be 5% of the purchase price of your home, that's a big chunk of change. Search for the best deal to save yourself as much money as possible.

- Closing at the end of the month is always better. If you choose to set your closing date at the beginning of the month, you'll end up paying more "prepaid interest," which is due at closing. Set your closing date as close to the end of the month as you can to avoid paying extra upon settling.

- Longer term mortgages cost more. If you talk to any mortgage lender, they'll try to push you towards a 30-year loan. You may think that this is because it's more affordable for you. While it will cost you less on a month-to-month basis, you'll end up paying quite a bit more in interest. If you can swing the extra money, shoot for a 15- or 20-year mortgage instead.

- There are ways to take a break from your mortgage payments. When times get tough and you are struggling to make your mortgage payment, you do have options beyond foreclosure and short sales. Most lenders offer skip-a-payment or forbearance options for those who qualify. Depending on the severity of your situation, you may even be eligible to have your payments suspended for a few months.

- Don't fall for gimmicks. Even if a lender advertises a no-cost closing, there's usually a catch. Depending on the circumstances, the lender may roll the closing costs into the loan. This means that you're actually paying more for the closing costs over the life of the loan due to interest. If it's not rolled into your loan, they may charge a higher interest rate—which would also cost you more over time.

- Most of the front line staff that you and the clients are dealing with are not home owners themselves and cannot provide you with a great scope of knowledge and information because they can't speak to you from experience. They are only trained to sell you the products the bank has to offer.

CREDIT

I Specialize in credit building and repairing. Credit to me is the most important aspect of a mortgage transaction. There are three vital parts when it comes to residential lending… the property, the credit and the income. You must have two out of three working for you to get an approval.

Credit is something that needs to be branded into every student's head before they leave elementary school. In my opinion it should be taught in grade eight. The reason being is not all students end up finishing high school. However, most kids tend to complete elementary. I think that if the average Canadian was taught how important credit is throughout their whole adult life, we would have a lot less people in a position with bad credit.

It hurts my inner being when I see someone with bruised credit, especially when they are for little issues (i.e. unpaid bills, late payments, etc.).

The biggest negative effect on one's credit is usually phone bills, as most people don't realize that yes, they are reported to your credit bureau.

If you are in a rough position, of being one of the unfortunate, misguided individuals who has been plagued by the credit system. give me a call and let's discuss your situation. There are still options available to you. Believe it or not, like insurance, everyone is entitled to a mortgage. However, just like auto insurance, you pay higher premiums when your records are bad. With mortgages you pay higher rates and higher fees when your credit is bad.

I often times advertise "No job, no credit, your approved!" This is another one of my many brand slogans, however, oftentimes, people think this applies to institutional mortgages. That is clearly not the case: the only time this is applicable is with a private mortgage.

When people approach me for a mortgage, the first thing I tell them to do is pull their credit report themselves then gather the required docs, so that we can review and work out a game plan… its beyond me to know the rate of people that stop the process, simply because they feel like I am making them do too much work. My mentor once told me, anything worth having is worth working hard for… so I empower you to follow my instructions, so we can build your financial future and make your dreams of homeownership a reality.

TEAM WORK

No man is an island… I plan on adopting this principle. I am so used to being a workaholic technician that it shows up in my brand "Call Andre." Hence the reason for the brand evolution into "CA Mortgage Group." We will re-engage that marketplace and bring awareness to the community, letting them know that Call Andre is now team, a force that is to be reckoned with, as we will stand together to serve and care for our clients, changing their lives one deal at a time.

I believe team work is important in all aspects of life, especially in the real estate market place. If you think about it, when you purchase a home, you have many people on your side working with you to get you from point A – Z. Your team consists of your mortgage broker, your realtor, your lawyer, your home inspector, your home appraiser and your financial planner

It's always good to make sure you have the best players on your side working on your best interest at all times. They should have one common goal: to serve and care for your needs and to make your experience an exceptional one. That is what we strive for here at **Call Andre at 1.647.991.7325.**

Step Into Greatness

LES BROWN

You have greatness within you. You can do more than you could ever imagine. The problem most people have is that they set a goal and then ask "how can I do it? I don't have the necessary skills or education or experience".

I know what that's like. I wasted 14 years on asking myself how I could be a motivational speaker. My mind focused on the negative—on the things that were in my way, rather than on the things that were not.

It's not what you don't have but what you think you need that keeps you from getting what you want from life. But, when the dream is big enough, the obstacles don't matter. You'll get there if you stay the course. Nothing can stop you but death itself.

Think about that last statement for a minute. There's nothing on this earth that can stop you from achieving what it is that you want. So, get out of your way, and quit sabotaging your dreams. Do everything in your power to make them happen—because you cannot fail!

They say the best way to die is with your loved ones gathered around your bed. But what if you were dying and it was the ideas you never acted upon, the gifts you never used and the dreams you never pursued, that were circled around your bed? Answer that question right now. Write down your answers. If you die this very moment what ideas, what gifts, what dreams will die with you?

Then say: I refuse to die an unlived life! You beat out 40 million sperm to get here, and you'll never have to face such odds again. Walk through the field of life and leave a trail behind.

One day, one of my rich friends brought my mother a new pair of shoes for me. Now, even though we weren't well off, I didn't want them; they were a size nine and I was a size nine and a half. My mother didn't listen and told my sister to go get some Vaseline, which she rubbed all over my feet. Then my mother had me put those shoes on, minding that I didn't scrunch down the heel. She had my sister run some water in the bathtub, and I was told to get in and walk around in the water. I said that my feet hurt. She just ignored me and asked about my day at school, how everything went and did I get into any fights? I knew what she was up to, that she was trying to distract me, so I said I had only gotten into three fights. After a while mother asked me if my feet still hurt. I admitted that the pain had indeed lessened. She kept me walking in that tub until I had a brand new pair of comfortable, size nine and a half shoes.

You see, once the leather in the shoes got wet, they stretched! And what you need to do is stretch a little. I believe that most people don't set high goals and miss them, but rather, they set lower goals and hit them and then they stay there, stuck on the side of the highway of life. When you're pursuing your greatness, you don't know what your limitations are, and you need to act like you don't have any. If you shoot for the moon and miss, you'll still be in the stars.

You also need coaching (a mentor). Why? There are times you, too, will find yourself parked on the side of the highway of life with no gas in the vehicle. What you need then is someone to stop and offer to pick up some gas down the road a ways and bring it back to you. That person is your coach. Yes, they are there for advice, but their main job is to help you through the difficulties that life throws at all of us.

Another reason for having a coach is that you can't see the picture when you're in the frame. In other words, he or she can often see where you are with a clarity and focus that's unavailable to you. They're not going to leave you parked along the road of life, nor are they going to allow you to be stuck in the moment like a photo in a frame.

And let's say you just can't see you're way forward. You don't believe it's possible. Sometimes you just have to believe in someone's belief in you. This could be your coach, a loved one or even a staunch friend. You need to hear them say you can do it, time and again. Because, after all, faith comes from hearing and hearing and hearing.

Look at it this way. Most people fail because of possibility blindness. They can't see what lies before them. There are always possibilities. Because of this, your dream is possible. You may fail often. In fact, I want you to say this: I will fail my way to success. Here is why.

I had a TV show that failed. I felt I had to go back to public speaking. I had failed, so I parked my car for ten years. Then I saw Dr. Wayne Dyer was still on PBS and I decided to call them. They said they would love to work with me and asked where I had been. I wasn't as good as I had been ten years before, as I was out of practice, but I still had to get back in the game. I was determined to drive on empty.

Listen to recordings, go to seminars, challenge yourself, and you'll begin to step into your greatness, you'll begin to fill yourself with the energy you need to climb to ever greater heights. Most people never attend a seminar. They won't invest money in books or audio programs. You put yourself in the top 5 percent just by making a different choice than the average person. This is called contrary thinking. It's a concept taken from the financial industry. One considers choosing the exact opposite behaviour of the average person as a way to get better than average results. You don't have to make the contrarian choice, but if you don't have anything to lose by going that road, why not consider the option?

Make your move before you're ready. Walk by faith not by sight and make sure you're happy doing it. If you can't be happy, what else is there? Helen Keller said, "Life is short, eat the dessert first."

What is faith? Many of us think of God when we think of faith. A different viewpoint claims that faith is a firm belief in something for which there is no proof. I would rather think of faith as something that is believed especially with strong conviction. It is this last definition I am referring to when I say walk by faith not by sight. Be happy and go forth with strong conviction that you are destined for greatness.

An important step on your way to greatness is to take the time to detoxify. You've got to look at the people in your life. What are they doing for you? Are they setting a pace that you can follow? If not, whose pace have you adjusted to? If you're the smartest in your group, find a new group.

Are the people in your life pulling you down or lifting you up? You know what to do, right? Banish the negative and stay with the positive; it's that simple. Dr. Norman Vincent Peale once said (when I was in the audience), "You are special. You have greatness within you, and you can do more than you could ever possibly imagine."

He overrode the inner conversations in my mind and reached the heart of me. He set me on fire. This is yet another reason for seeking out the help of a coach or mentor or other new people in your life. They can do what Dr. Peale did for me. They can set your passion free.

How important is it to have the right kind of person/people on your side? There was a study done that determined it takes 16 people saying you can do something to overcome one person who says you can't do something. That's right, one negative, unsupportive person can wipe out the work of 16 other supportive people. The message can't be any clearer than that.

Let's face the cold, hard truth: most people stay in park along the highway of life. They never feel the passion, the love for their fellow man, or for the work they do. They are stuck in the proverbial rut. What's the reason? There are many reasons, but only one common factor: fear — fear of change, fear of failure, fear of success, fear they may not be good enough, fear of competition, even fear of rejection.

"Rejection is a myth," says Jack Canfield, co-author of The Chicken Soup for the Soul series. "It's not like you get a slap in the face each time you are rejected." Why not take every "no" you receive as a vitamin, and every time you take one know you are another step closer to success.

You will win if you don't quit. Even a broken clock is right twice a day.

Professional baseball players, on average, get on base just three times out of every ten times they face the opposing pitcher. Even superstars fail half of the time they appear at the plate.

Top commissioned salespeople face similar odds. They make may make one sale from every three people they see, but it will have taken them between 75 and 100 telephone calls to make the 15 appointments they need to close their five sales for the week. And these are statistics for the elite. Most salespeople never reach these kinds of numbers.

People don't spend their lives working for just one company anymore. This means you must build up a set of skills and experiences that are portable. This can be done a number of ways, but my favourite approaches follow.

You must be willing to do the things others won't do in order to have tomorrow the things that others don't have. Provide more service than you get paid for. Set some high standards for yourself.

Begin each day with your most difficult task. The rest of the day will seem more enjoyable and a whole lot easier.

Someone needs help with a problem? Be the solution to that problem.

Also, find those tasks that are being consistently ignored and do them. You'll be surprised by the results. An acquaintance of mine used this approach at a number of entry-level positions and each time he quickly ended up being offered a position in management.

You must increase your energy. Kick it up a notch. We are spirits having a physical existence; let your spirit shine. Quit frittering away your energy. Use it to move you closer to the achievement of your dreams. Refuse to spend it on non-productive activities.

What do people say about you when you leave a room? Are you willing to take responsibility—to walk your talk. There is a terrible epidemic sweeping our nation, and it is the refusal to take responsibility for one's actions. Consider that at some point in any situation there will have been a moment where you could have done something to change the outcome. To that end you are responsible for what happened. It's a hard thing to accept, but it's true.

Life's hard. It was hard when I was told I had cancer. I had sunken into despair, and was hiding away in my study when my son came in. My son asked me if I was going to die. What could I do? I told him I was going to fight, even though I was scared. I also told him that I needed some help. Not because I was weak but because I wanted to stay strong. Keep asking until you get help. Don't stop until you get it.

A setback is the setup for a comeback. A setback is simply a misstep on the long road of success. It means nothing in the larger scheme of things. And, surprisingly, it sets you up for your next win. It tends to focus you and your energy on your immediate goals, paving the way for your next sprint, for your comeback.

It's worth it. Your dreams are worth the sacrifices you'll have to make to achieve them. Find five reasons that will make your dreams worth it for you. Say to yourself, I refuse to live an unlived life.

If you are casual about your dreams, you'll end up a casualty. You must be passionate about your dreams, living and breathing them throughout your days. You've got to be hungry! People who are hungry refuse to take no for an answer. Make NO your vitamin. Be unstoppable. Be hungry.

Let me give you an example of what I mean by hungry ...

I decided I wanted to become a disc jockey, so I went down to the local radio station and asked the manager, Mr. Milton "Butterball" Smith, if he had a job available for a disc jockey. He said he did not. The next day I went back, and Mr. Smith asked "Weren't you here yesterday?" I explained that I was just checking to see if anyone was sick or had died. He responded by telling me not to come back again. Day three, I went back again—with the same story. Mr. Smith told me to get out of there. I came back the fourth day and gave Mr. Smith my story one more time. He was so beside himself that he told me to get him a cup of coffee. I said, "Yes, sir!" That's how I became the errand boy.

While working as an errand boy at the station, I took every opportunity to hang out with the deejays and to observe them working. After I had taught myself how to run the control room, it was just a matter of biding my time.

Then one day an opportunity presented itself. One of the disc jockeys by the name of Rockin' Roger was drinking heavily while he was on the air. It was a Saturday afternoon. And there I was, the only one there.

I watched him through the control-room window. I walked back and forth in front of that window like a cat watching a mouse, saying "Drink, Rock, Drink!" I was young. I was ready. And I was hungry.

Pretty soon, the phone rang. It was the station manager. He said, "Les, this is Mr. Klein."

I said, "Yes, I know."

He said, "Rock can't finish his program."

I said, "Yes sir, I know."

He said, "Would you call one of the other disc jockeys to fill in?"

I said, "Yes sir, I sure will, sir."

And when he hung up, I said, "Now he must think I'm crazy." I called up my mama and my girlfriend, Cassandra, and I told them, "Ya'll go out on the front porch and turn up the radio, I'M ABOUT TO COME ON THE AIR!"

I waited 15 or 20 minutes and called the station manager back. I said, "Mr. Klein, I can't find NOBODY!"

He said, "Young boy, do you know how to work the controls?"

I said, "Yes, sir."

He said, "Go in there, but don't say anything. Hear me?"

I said, "Yes, sir."

I couldn't wait to get old Rock out of the way. I went in there, took my seat behind that turntable, flipped on the microphone and let 'er rip.

"Look out, this is me, LB., triple P. Les Brown your platter-playin' papa. There were none before me and there will be none after me, therefore that makes me the one and only. Young and single and love to mingle, certified, bona fide and indubitably qualified to bring you satisfaction and a whole lot of action. Look out baby, I'm your LOVE man."

I WAS HUNGRY!

During my adult life I've been a deejay, a radio station manager, a Democrat in the Ohio Legislature, a minister, a TV personality, an author and a public speaker, but I've always looked after what I valued most—my mother. What I want for her is one of my dreams, one of my goals.

My life has been a true testament to the power of positive thinking and the infinite human potential. I was born in an abandoned building on a floor in Liberty City, a low-income section of Miami, Florida, and adopted at six weeks of age by Mrs. Mamie Brown, a 38-year-old single woman, cafeteria cook and domestic worker. She had very little education or financial means, but a very big heart and the desire to care for myself and my twin brother. I call myself Mrs. Mamie Brown's Baby Boy and I say that all that I am and all that I ever hoped to be, I owe to my mother.

My determination and persistence in searching for ways to help my mother overcome poverty and developing my philosophy to do whatever it takes to achieve success led me to become a distinguished authority on harnessing human potential and success. That philosophy is best expressed by the following …

> "If you want a thing bad enough to go out and fight for it,
> to work day and night for it,
> to give up your time, your peace and your sleep for it…
> if all that you dream and scheme is about it,
> and life seems useless and worthless without it…
> if you gladly sweat for it and fret for it and plan for it
> and lose all your terror of the opposition for it…
> if you simply go after that thing you want
> with all of your capacity, strength and sagacity,
> faith, hope and confidence and stern pertinacity…
> if neither cold, poverty, famine, nor gout,
> sickness nor pain, of body and brain,
> can keep you away from the thing that you want…
> if dogged and grim you beseech and beset it,
> with the help of God, you will get it!"

The 3 Things You Need to Become a Real Estate Millionaire

The Right Way to Invest Successfully

RAYMOND AARON

I
t seems like everywhere you look, someone is claiming that they became a millionaire by investing in real estate, and encouraging you to do the same. There are lots of TV shows about flipping houses for a fast buck that make it appear as if it's easy to find the right property and just as easy to sell it in a matter of months for a good profit. Unfortunately, that's not really how it works.

Investing in real estate is a proven way to make money, a lot of it. You could end up with millions, but you could also make a lot of very costly mistakes along the way. There has been so much hype about how easy it is to become a real estate millionaire that many people jump into the market without knowing what they are doing, and that's a shame, especially because qualified help is available.

Anyone can invest successfully in real estate if they have three things: a great real estate mentor, a proven real estate system, and a way to correctly predict the future. In other words, you need someone smart and knowledgeable to guide you, an understanding of the financial and legal aspects of buying, holding and selling real estate, and an ability to see societal trends and visualize how those trends will impact the real estate market.

A GREAT REAL ESTATE MENTOR

Investing on your own can be financially dangerous, especially for a first-timer. You're dealing with a lot of money, so any mistake can be a huge one. Buying at the wrong time in the cycle can kill your investments. And, regardless of the real estate strategy you employ, you're bound to hold onto properties for some period of time which means that severe negative cash flow and vacancies can ruin you. Plus, bad property management and a failure to know the most recent real estate and tax laws can get you sued.

An experienced mentor can help you choose the best real estate strategies for your situation, and the right properties in which to invest. They can also help you avoid the many possible pitfalls and make money while holding properties, and counsel you on when to sell for a great profit. Working with the right mentor can also keep real estate investing from becoming your full-time job.

Many people find that some part of the investment process is uncomfortable for them, whether it's initiating a conversation with a realtor, submitting an offer or hiring a property manager. A mentor can be very helpful in such situations as well.

In sum, learning from and working with the right mentor can make you a highly profitable investor in a relatively short period of time. Look for someone with years of experience and a proven track record.

A PROVEN SYSTEM

There's much more to investing in real estate than "buy low, sell high." To be successful, you must have the correct facts and the correct monthly habits concerning your real estate. Overall, you need to know what to buy, when to buy it, whether there will be a positive cash flow while you're holding on to it, and when to sell. Plus, what is the right low? What is the right high? How much money do you have to put down and how much income must be generated while you're waiting to sell?

Determining if a property is a good buy takes a lot of research and analysis. You will need to look at comparable purchase prices in the area, as well as rental fees. You'll also need to consider the location, the age and condition of the building, tax rates and about 30 other pieces of data. Evaluating the information for just one property could take you a day or more.

If you're serious about becoming a real estate investor, you are going to be considering quite a lot of properties on a regular basis. Even if you want to make investing your day job, you'll never have the time necessary to research fully and evaluate every property that comes to your attention. Hence, the first part of your system has to involve weeding out the lesser opportunities and focusing on the ones with potential.

The investors I mentor learn how to determine if a property is really a great deal in seconds. You only need two pieces of data: the purchase price and the current rent rate. Compare the two using a two-part formula. First, divide the asking price (outgoing funds) by 100. Then, given that current mortgage interest rates are below 8-10% divide the number you got by two. If the current monthly rent doesn't meet or better that second number, eliminate the property from consideration.

As an example, say the asking price is $1 million. If you divide it by 100, it comes out to $10 thousand. Divide again, by two, and you get $5 thousand. If the monthly rent isn't $5 thousand or more, you should pass on the property. You may miss out on a few winners using this system but, if you eliminate more properties than you think you should, you'll be successful and safe. Remember that, if interest rates rise significantly, you will need to adjust the formula to compensate.

Once you've weeded out the chaff from the wheat, do your due diligence on the remaining properties. Work closely with your mentor during this part of the process and, again, when it comes to making deals, say no more than you say yes. Just don't get cold feet or shy away from a great deal.

In terms of timing, it all comes down to momentum. There is always an overall upward momentum. Real estate prices go up and down, on an upwards track. So, one good profit strategy is to buy low, watch values rise and sell during the next boom. More precisely, you want to buy just as prices rise off the bottom (so that they're already rising) and sell when prices hit double the bottom, which is typically the very minimum prices rise to at the peak of the ensuing boom.

Don't attempt to predict the extremes — you will make a significant amount of money more safely buying just after prices begin rising (not the lowest point) and selling towards the end of the up period —without the risk associated with waiting too long and missing the highest point.

You'll also need a system for monitoring your investments while holding on until it's time to sell. Having a strong property manager is essential. So is reviewing rents taken in versus uncollectibles, repairs, and other expenses to ensure that your cash flow remains positive.

PREDICTING THE FUTURE

Good real estate investors learn to identify marketplace trends and buyers' or renters' needs. Start by investigating and tracking growth trends by neighborhood: are prices rising, is an area getting ready for a renaissance, are there new job opportunities nearby or is the area close to another neighborhood that's gotten too pricey?

Great real estate investors, however, go far beyond those basics. They look for large demographic or social elements that might provide the next big opportunity. The huge number of returning veterans after World War II led to a Baby Boom that provides the perfect example. Every stage of their lives brought an opportunity for marketers, real estate builders, and other manufacturers to fill unmet needs, be it starter homes for when they had children, tricycles for those children who were too young to ride a bike, or new sizes and types of cars. All of this was predictable, but no one noticed. Opportunities were capitalized upon as they arose, but imagine what financial success could have been attained if someone had predicted the Baby Boomers' needs in advance.

And, now, those Boomers are driving the growth of retirement communities and nursing homes. But, they are a more independent lot than their parents were, and have strived to remain young and healthy as long as possible. Quite a few of them can still live and thrive on their own, but many may need a little help at this point in their lives. They don't need or want an aide, nurse or social worker on a full-time basis and certainly aren't ready for a nursing home. That means there is a huge need for more up-to-date, internet-ready independent supportive living arrangements, of which there are too few. Investing in one now is bound to be a win.

Don't forget that those Baby Boomers had children of their own, and that created a mini baby boom. Think about the ways in which those children, now middle-aged adults, are different from their parents and what needs they might have, especially regarding real estate. You might also consider whether changes in the workforce, higher divorce rates and the economics of leaving home after college have implications for the real estate market as well. Keep your eyes and minds open!

If you would like to learn more about winning strategies for investing in real estate, please visit http://rarestmonthlymentor.com.

Sex, Love and Relationships

DR. JOHN GRAY

J ust as great sex is important to lasting love, good health is important to sex and relationships. About 12 years ago, I cured myself of early stage Parkinson's disease. The doctors were amazed, but my wife was even more amazed. She noted that our relationship and sex life had become dramatically better. It turns out that the natural supplements I used to reverse Parkinson's can also make you more attentive and loving in your relationship. At that point, I realized that good relationship skills alone were not enough to sustain love and passion for a lifetime.

I shared many insights gained from my 40 years' experience as a marriage counselor and coach in *Men Are From Mars, Women Are From Venus*. And while my insights go a long way towards helping men and women understand and support each other, good communication skills alone are not always enough. For better relationships, we not only need to be healthy, but we must also experience optimum brain function.

If you are tired, depressed, anxious, not sleeping well, or in pain, then certainly romantic feelings will become a thing of the past. My recovery from Parkinson's revealed to me the profound connection between the quality of our health and our relationships. This insight has motivated me, over the past twelve years, to research the secrets of optimum health as a foundation for lasting love.

These are health secrets that are generally not explored in medical school. In medical school, doctors are indoctrinated into the culture of examining the symptoms, identifying the sickness, and prescribing a drug to treat that sickness. They learn very little about how to be healthy or to sustain successful relationships.

There are no university courses entitled "Better Nutrition For Better Sex". Drugs sometimes save lives, but they also have negative side effects that do little to preserve the passion in a relationship. Ideally, drugs should be used as a last resort and 90 % of our health plan should be drug free. From this perspective, the heath care crisis, as well as our high rate of divorce in America, is indirectly caused by our dependence on doctors and prescription drugs.

Most people have not even considered that taking prescribed drugs (even for the small stuff) can weaken their relationships, which in turn makes them more vulnerable to more disease. For example, if you are feeling depressed or anxious, a drug may numb your pain, but it does nothing to help you correct the cause of your problem. It can even prevent you from feeling your natural motivation to get the emotional support you need. In a variety of ways, our common health complaints are all expressions of two major conditions: our lack of education to identify and support unmet gender-specific emotional needs; and our lack of education to identify and support unmet gender-specific nutritional needs.

With an understanding of natural solutions that have been around for thousands of years, drugs are not needed to treat many common complaints. Some symptoms like low energy, weight gain, allergies, hormonal imbalance, mood swings, poor sleep, indigestion, lack of focus, ADD and ADHD, procrastination, low motivation, memory loss, decreased libido, PMS, vaginal dryness, muscle and joint pain, or the lack of passion in life and/or our relationships can be treated drug-free. By using drugs (even over-the-counter drugs) to treat these common complaints, our bodies and relationships are weakened, making us more vulnerable to bigger and more costly health challenges like cancer, diabetes, heart disease, auto-immune disease, dementia, and Alzheimer's. In simple terms, by handling the easy stuff (the common complaints) without doctors and drugs, we can protect ourselves from the big stuff (cancer, heart disease, dementia, etc.) We can be healthy and also enjoy lasting love and passion in our personal lives.

Even if you are taking anti-depressants or hormone replacement therapy, sometimes all it takes to stop treating the symptom is to directly handle the cause. With specific mineral orotates (something most people have never heard of) or omega three oil from the brains of salmon, your stress levels immediately drop and you begin to feel happy and in love again.

For every health challenge, we have explored the effects on our relationships, with as well as natural remedies that can sometimes produce immediate positive results. You can find these natural solutions to common health complaints for free at my website: www.MarsVenus.com.

What they don't teach in medical school is how to be healthy and happy without the use of drugs or hormone replacement. By refusing drugs and taking responsibility for your health, a wealth of new possibilities can become available to you. We are designed to be healthy and happy, and it is within our reach if we commit to increasing our knowledge.

New research regarding the brain differences in men and women reveals how specific nutritional supplements, combined with gender-specific relationship and self-nurturing skills, can stimulate the hormones of health, happiness and increased energy. Over the past 10 years in my healing center in California, I witnessed how natural solutions coupled with gender-specific relationship skills could solve our common health complaints without drugs. By addressing these common complaints without prescribed drugs, not only do we feel better, but our relationships have the potential to improve dramatically.

Ultimately the cause of all our common complaints is higher stress levels. Researchers around the world all agree that chronic stress levels in our bodies provide a basis for any and all disease to take hold. An easy and quick solution for lowering our stress reactions is specific nutritional support combined with gender-smart relationship skills. Extra nutritional support is needed because stress depletes the body very quickly of essential nutrients. When a car engine is running more quickly, it uses fuel more quickly. When we are stressed, we need both extra nutrients and extra emotional support. Understanding what we need to take and where to get it requires education. Every week day at www.MarsVenus.com I have a live daily show where I freely answer questions and provide this much-needed new gender-specific insight.

At www.MarsVenus.com, we are happy to share what we have learned for creating healthy bodies and positive relationships. You can find a host of natural solutions for common complaints and feel confident that you have the power to feel fully alive with an abundance of energy and positive feelings that will enrich all your relationships.

Real Estate Isn't Just A Man's Game

5 Key Tips for Women Investors

CORA CRISTOBAL

Are you someone who wants to start investing in real estate, but doesn't know where to start? Are you someone who's trying to get back into it after failing at it once? Are you a semi-experienced investor looking to improve your returns?

If you answered "yes" to any of the above questions, then I commend you! Real estate investing is a very rewarding field, as long as you know what you're doing. In fact, at the lowest point in my life, the real estate market helped me get back on my feet and turn my life around for good.

Approximately ten years ago, I divorced my husband. Since his income was nearly twice as much as mine, our separation meant that I had to start living a lot more scarcely, until I could find a way to replace the income that he provided for me. And that's precisely what I did.

I started by transforming my basement into a pair of makeshift bedrooms so that I could rent them out at a profit. Once I got the hang of that, I invested in condos in Canada, rented them for income, and then flipped them for a profit after a few years. Then, I bought cheap American properties and rented those out, expanding my income even more. Before long, I had worked my way up to other money-making opportunities, and I was living more comfortably. As of now, I'm even better off than when I was married.

To me, real estate wasn't just a source of income, but a source of proof that I didn't have to depend on a man to live the life I wanted. On top of that, I proved that a single woman is perfectly capable of making it in a male-dominated industry.

Ultimately, I decided that my divorce wasn't going to be the end of my life; it was going to be a new beginning. And it can be a new beginning for you, too!

But that doesn't mean that real estate investing is easy. In fact, there are several pitfalls that I've seen countless novice investors fall into. Before you start your new career path, you should familiarize yourself with the most common (and often the most dangerous) mistakes made by new investors, so that you can avoid making them yourself.

MISTAKE #1
FALLING IN LOVE WITH THE PROPERTY

One thing you have to keep in mind is that you're looking for a property to rent out, not a property to live in. You need to look for the neighborhood that's experiencing the greatest demand, rather than the one that's most suited to your tastes.

The metrics you would use to choose a property to live in aren't identical to the metrics you'd use to choose one to rent. True, both decisions involve choosing a property that's centered in a good neighborhood, with close proximity to decent schools, shopping centers, and hospitals. However, there are several factors that are relevant to renters but not to buyers. Return on Investment (ROI), for instance, is the ratio between the income you receive from rent payments and the cost of the property. In other words, it measures how much you'll earn from the property compared to how much you had to pay for it. (If you were simply looking for a place to live, this wouldn't be a concern.)

By the same token, qualities that you look for in a home may not necessarily be qualities that make it rentable. If you plan on having children, you may base your judgment on whether the home is suitable for raising a family. As an investor, however, this cannot become the deciding factor in your decision, since a home without enough space for a four-person family can still be perfectly rentable to a single woman, a recent college graduate or an elderly couple. Don't limit your options.

Furthermore, you can't let yourself get too attached to the property you're investing in. You have to keep reminding yourself that, ultimately, you're going to have to part ways with the house and leave it in the hands of somebody else.

The point is, the factors that need to be at the front of your mind are the ones that determine whether the property can be rented out at a profit. Remember, you're not looking for a house that's good for you; you're looking for a property that's appealing to the average consumer.

MISTAKE #2
DISREGARDING SHORT-TERM CASH FLOW

When you're choosing a property to buy to rent, you may be tempted to look at projections on whether the property is expected to appreciate in value over time. That's fine if you want to keep the information in the back of your mind, but it shouldn't be your first priority. That needs to be short-term passive, positive cash flow, or how much you'll earn from rent payments in the coming months.

After all, making money through a resale requires time. It can take years or even decades for a house to appreciate significantly in value. In the meantime, you're going to need a way to feed, clothe and sustain yourself on a day-to-day basis.

Furthermore, projections aren't guarantees. There are so many different factors outside of our control that affect the housing market; nobody, not even experts like myself, can say with absolute certainty what a house's value will be ten to twenty years from now. Why base your decision on a projected increase in profit that could very well be nullified by a downturn in the market that nobody saw coming?

There's nothing wrong with planning for the far future per se, but planning for the near future is considerably more important. It's better to go for a smaller reward that you're guaranteed to receive immediately than to go for a large reward that you may or may not receive after a while. Remember, a bird in the hand is worth two in the bush.

MISTAKE #3
STARTING TOO BIG

Let's say you want to teach yourself how to cook. You don't start with fancy, elaborate recipes that take hours to prepare, do you? Of course not; you'd just end up ruining your dinner or even your kitchen. Instead, you start with simple recipes, and once you've mastered those, you gradually work your way up to the harder stuff.

Why should real estate investing be any different? All too often, I've seen new investors immediately set their eyes on fancy, expensive multi-million dollar properties. While those kinds of properties have a chance of offering a huge return for you, it's also incredibly likely that you'll suffer a huge loss, especially if you don't have the discerning, savvy eye of an experienced investor.

Instead, start by investing in smaller properties within the $100K-$500K range. In fact, you can start even smaller than that by renting out rooms in your living space (like I did). Some investors start by purchasing a small duplex property to live in and then renting out one of the units to someone else, thus fulfilling their need for a source of income and a roof over their head at the same time.

Then, once you've saved up enough money from rent payments, you can work your way up to larger houses. Slowly, but surely, you can increase the value of what you buy, and consequently, increase your income. As I mentioned above, that was how I broke into the real estate industry, and it worked wonders for me.

Of course, if you don't trust your own judgment, you may be interested in forming a partnership with another investor. Which leads me to my next point.

MISTAKE #4
CHOOSING THE WRONG PARTNER

A partnership, on its own, isn't a bad idea; in fact, it can be a very good one. There are lots of advantages to forming a partnership with another investor. Ideally, you'll have someone with whom to share the workload, and an extra source of knowledge and expertise. Plus, you'll have the potential to make more capital without investing as much of your personal funds or getting too much credit.

Note, however, that I said "ideally." In a worst-case scenario, you'll end up with a partner who never does their share, makes bad decisions on your behalf, and almost ruins your chances of ever making it as an investor. If you want to avoid that (and I assume that you do), there are a few things you will have to keep in mind before you decide to make your partnership official.

First of all, if you plan on forming a partnership with someone else, it needs to be someone who knows what they're doing, or at least someone who doesn't know any less than you do. Check their credentials and see if they have any background in real estate or any form of investment planning. If you're new to the field, you don't want to end up in a "blind leading the blind" situation.

Second of all, you have to find someone whose goals are more or less the same as yours. Remember, your primary objective is maximizing passive, positive cash flow, so make sure that your partner's looking for the same thing. Otherwise, it'll be almost impossible to find an investment plan that satisfies both your needs.

For this reason, I strongly suggest putting every agreement in writing. Discuss every course of action thoroughly, and once you reach a consensus, put it down on a piece of paper and sign it. I've seen too many partners mistakenly assume that they were "on the same page," only to pay dearly for it later.

Furthermore, holding regular discussions is a great way to familiarize yourself with the field. You'll be exposed to a separate point of view, you'll learn to use real estate lingo properly, and most importantly, you'll end up making better decisions than you would have on your own. Two heads are better than one, after all.

MISTAKE #5
GOING IN WITHOUT A MENTOR

A partner is, for all intents and purposes, your equal, and she has a direct stake in your decision-making process. For a truly reliable source of guidance, you're going to need someone far more knowledgeable than yourself, who can evaluate your situation from a non-biased perspective.

I may have accomplished a lot, but I didn't get to where I am entirely on my own, although I tried. For several years, I tried to tackle the real estate industry alone, and as a result, things didn't go as smoothly as I had hoped. In fact, many of the mistakes I've outlined in this chapter are mistakes that I made in my early years. Things improved for me when I hired a mentor. He had experience investing in both Canada and the United States, and he was willing to share all of the high and low points of his career with me: the failures and successes. By telling me of his failures, he taught me what to avoid doing as an investor. By telling me of his successes, he imbued me with the confidence to carry on; if he could do it, I could do it too.

After a few years of meeting with my mentor twice a month, I had both the knowledge to avoid making bad decisions and the confidence to make good ones. Also, I was able to invest in my personal growth and development. I established and improved my brand; that contributed largely to my success.

I'm proud of my success, but I would have earned it a lot sooner if I had hired a mentor from the very beginning. So, don't repeat the biggest mistake I made in my career — starting without a muse.

If you're interested in learning more about my coaching, mentoring or consulting services, please visit www.TorontoWomensClub.com or feel free to contact me at cora.cristobal@gmail.com.

Nobody Got Time For That!

The Ultimate Guide For Smart Money Management

URSULA GARRETT

S ave, save, save! That's all you hear from family, friends and the media. You are strongly encouraged to save, but how are you supposed to save with a low-paying job, high student loan debt, and the rising cost of housing? Something has got to give – and it's usually not you giving to your savings account. Who has time to be broke when you are young and just want to have fun and enjoy your life? I'll tell you who – nobody. Nobody has got time for that, especially you!

Finances absolutely play a huge part in your life choices and opportunities. Money issues consume chunks of your brain power every day. Think of how many times money (or a lack of it) factors into your decisions throughout your fast-paced day. For instance, you schedule a date on Tinder, buy movie tickets on Fandango and make dinner reservation using Open Table, and you haven't even gotten out of bed yet to start your day. You can do this if you have money in your bank account or power (available credit) on your credit card. Yes, either method of payment will get you what you want right now – one is a smart choice and the other, not so much. You must make smart choices regularly, there is no getting around it.

Size does matter, especially when it refers to your bank account. I want you to recognize that money underwrites the type of life you live and the lack of it means you're not living the life you want to be living. You are forced to make hard choices about what you can afford or what you have to give up. Having limited options make you feel as if your life is less than it could be. Smart money management is the key to your financial goals and personal goals aligning.

Once you recognize that the choices you make with your finances are either limiting your options or providing you opportunities, you can start being more proactive with your finances. First, it is important for you to understand how easy it is to handle your personal business, so you can create real changes that will significantly impact your life.

Two of my five daughters are about the same age, 26 (not twins just a blended family). Throughout their lives, they have taken different paths and made different choices. They are in their mid-twenties now and both spend more than they should, however, one is contributing to a retirement plan and has money go directly from her paycheck into a savings account. The other one lives paycheck to paycheck, has no retirement savings, no personal savings, and is regularly subsidized by her parents. Three guesses which one has more opportunities to live the life she wants, and the first two guesses don't count. While they each had similar opportunities, their individual choices have dictated their current circumstances.

"I am not a product of my circumstances. I am a product of my decisions."

- Stephen Covey

It's a bit of a mystery why you make some of the decisions you make and that's especially true when it comes to your finances. I can tell you from experience that a crystal ball, mesmerizing though it may be, is not where you will find those answers. How often have you made poor financial choices in the moment, only to later regret them and wonder how you got into this situation again? Well, I'm here to tell you that it doesn't matter how or why, what matters is what you do to fix it and make sure it never happens again.

If you have ever paid attention to political elections, then you know how easily you can be fooled by your assumptions, fears and false intuitions. I say this to help you understand that listening to others' opinions about what you should do won't help you reach your goals. Making a plan and following through will.

Which is why I find it useful to understand some principle concepts when you make decisions about money. This is besides, of course, the regular practices of following a budget, saving, investing and avoiding most kinds of debt, factors that I will discuss as part of the steps for smart money management.

These four concepts are the foundation you need for your decision-making process when you are creating your budget or making the decisions about those investments and savings plans. They need to factor into all your financial decisions, because they will help keep you from sabotaging your financial stability.

1) OPPORTUNITY COSTS

No matter what you do or the opportunities that you pursue, there is always going to be a cost. You have to give something to get something. Nothing in life is free. Individually, we get to decide what we are willing to give in exchange. In some circumstances, the price is simply too high, or the payoff is too low to make the deal or take the chance. That threshold is different for everyone and is based on your values.

For example, deciding whether or not to pursue higher education is a decision you make based on your priorities, which could include your financials, your time, and your perception of the value of higher education. Pursuing an advanced degree may take years -- are you willing to put in that amount of time? It could involve giving up other opportunities to finish your degree, but at the same time, the network you build could allow you access to individuals who can create even greater career opportunities in the future. Many individuals choose their university based on the alumni and the type of network they can access for mentors.

Additionally, there is the debt that often comes with pursuing higher education. Are you willing to put yourself into that kind of debt, the type of debt that will take years to pay off? Many individuals see their degree as a doorway to career advancement in a specific field or as a way to pursue the type of work that they are passionate about. For them, the cost of the degree in terms of finances and time is worth it, because they see that degree as an investment in their long-term financial future.

Those two daughters I mentioned earlier, one went to college and has a degree in business and some student loan debt. The other worked part-time jobs and traveled to visit friends she met on the internet. One daughter wanted a college degree and was willing to sacrifice four years of her life, accumulate debt (she considered it as an investment) and forego immediate travel opportunities. The other daughter thought that price was too high. This isn't a matter of right or wrong but a matter of what you are willing to give to get what you want. Here is a general rule of thumb: The bigger the opportunity, the greater the cost or sacrifice to achieve it.

Every decision that you make has all those considerations and it is up to you to give them all a voice before you make your decision. At the same time, your priorities need to guide those smaller financial decisions that we all make throughout the day. Many of your long-term goals are going to be impacted by your short-term decisions. Therefore, giving yourself guidelines for daily spending based on your priorities will help you to reach those goals. Still, not everything can be quantified in terms of your return on investment, as I will explore next.

2) SUNK COSTS

What is sunk cost? This is money you can't get back -- a non-refundable airline ticket, for example. There are certain expenses that you will have throughout your life that are not going to bring a tangible return on investment. In fact, they are likely going to result in nothing more than an enjoyable experience or a pleasant memory. It can be easy to get into a mindset that has you spending far beyond what you may have budgeted or prioritized because you value the experience, but it can put you in a financial bind later. The idea here is that you need to keep sunk costs in proper perspective. It's easy to start thinking, "Well, I've already spent $100, so what's another $25?" My mother always told me not to throw good money after bad. She taught me to understand the concept of sunk costs long before I took a business class. You have got to be willing to walk away sometimes and keep the money in your pocket for other investment opportunities.

Once something is paid for, and cannot be refunded, it shouldn't impact your future financial decisions. It is a "sunk" cost, i.e. water under the bridge, and no matter what you do in the future you won't ever get it back. Therefore, you can't allow yourself to get hung up on the moments where you spent money in a way that didn't fall into your overall financial plan. In the end, you have to accept that sunk costs are going to happen and make your peace with them. Recognize that you will buy emotionally and defend rationally, even if that might not always be wise. There are costs that are simply not recoupable.

Regrets over sunk costs can make it harder to move forward, leaving you vulnerable to make other choices that you may not have otherwise made. Do not allow yourself to fall into the downward spiral. Negative thoughts often breed more negative thoughts, especially if you continue to dwell on them. The same can be said for financial decisions. When you focus on your bad financial decisions, you may find yourself repeating them, because that is your focus.

It is important to keep yourself focused on ways to improve your financial decisions and keep them in line with your financial plan. Yes, you might regret a decision, but make the conscious choice not to dwell on it. Instead, learn from it and move forward. Life, especially when it comes to finances, is a series of learning experiences. The better you are at accepting the lessons, the better decisions you will be able to make in the future. I find inspiration and humor in the lyrics of one of my favorite songs by Chumbawamba, "I get knocked down, but I get up again, you're never gonna keep me down."

Now that you have that mindset (and that song stuck in your head), you can keep yourself from making financial decisions based on your sunk costs and focus on maximizing your earnings. That starts by focusing on finding the right investments for you. With that in mind, let's talk about the Rule of 72.

3) QUICK INTEREST CALCULATIONS USING THE RULE OF 72

One of your biggest concerns about an investment should be, "What am I going to get out of this?" While you wouldn't want to ask that of a date, it's perfectly acceptable, in fact it's expected, to ask that of a potential investment. All of us want a way to determine the upside of a financial opportunity. Now there are several ways to analyze a financial investment, but it often comes down to how long it will take for an investment to pay off. Want to double your holdings? The Rule of 72 can tell you how long it will take, based on the specific interest rate. Just divide 72 by the interest rate to learn how long it will take to double your initial investment.

For example, if you are looking at an investment with an interest rate of 6 percent, then 72 divided by 6 gets you 12 years. You can then take that information and use it to determine if that timeframe will work with your overall financial plan. Granted, you may find that other factors will play a part in determining your return as well, but it is important to have an idea of what you can expect before you put money into an investment.

This is a rough estimate, of course, but it's pretty effective. Recognize that you might find that a return is going to take significantly longer to make you money. So even if you find it an interesting opportunity, you may opt to not invest in order to take advantage of a different opportunity that will give you a faster return on your money.

In fact, you can also turn the equation around to determine the interest rate you are looking at if someone promises to double your returns in a set amount of time. Twice as much money in 12 years? Divide 72 by 12 and you get an interest rate of 6 percent. This rule lets you evaluate investment opportunities quickly and decide where to put your money in a way that will help you to grow your investments to meet long-term financial goals.

Keep in mind, future earnings are not something that you can count on, so how you use the dollars that you have now are going to have greater weight than potential earnings. You know that old saying, "Don't count your chickens before the eggs hatch."

4) THE TIME VALUE OF MONEY

According to this concept, a dollar you receive today is worth more than a dollar you will get tomorrow. You will have opportunity to invest that dollar immediately and begin earning more revenue from it (and also avoid losing value because of inflation).

It is important to recognize that money from your investments needs to be put to work. Don't be quick to spend it. Making frivolous or useless purchases means you are making a choice to spend on meaningless things and activities and in doing so, you are draining your ability to invest and grow. Focus on how you can essentially create a chain of investments, all working to grow an income stream for you to use in retirement or even for a big purchase that is part of your financial plan (think a house or car). Growth is a long-term process and it is imperative that you do make the time for it.

When you are waiting for an investment to pay off, then you are waiting for your money to work for you. One of the ways that you can save money is by limiting your interest payments. When you are making money from investments, which is then reinvested, you create an income stream that can allow you to pay cash for items, or put down a larger down payment, thus helping to reduce those interest payments, or eliminate them altogether.

Again, this helps you make certain calls about your purchases -- and your income. It's the old "one bird in the hand is worth two in a bush" theory in action for your wallet.

These four concepts have served me well over the years. Now let's focus in on the five steps that will help you to remain financially sound as you invest and grow your income to meet your financial goals.

WHY MONEY MATTERS

Before I talk about the steps, I want you to understand that money has a place and purpose in your life. Whatever adventures or experiences you want to have, you are going to need money to do it. That money is also going to be a key part of fulfilling your life's purpose, simply because money is a resource that can help you get things done. Regardless of if your goal in life is to have a non-profit that helps others or to create a company to bring a product or process to market, the truth is that money will be a resource that you need.

Since you and I can agree on that, let's start talking about your financial goals by first talking about your life goals.

STEP 1 - BUDGETING: YOUR PERSONAL BUSINESS PLAN

You have goals you want to accomplish, experience, and create in this life. This is simply a reality we all share. By defining your goals, you are able to determine what financial moves are necessary to achieve them. Too often, personal goals are overlooked or under-appreciated when creating a financial plan. Your personal goals and your financial plan need to be in sync for you to be successful at achieving either one.

For instance, if you know that your financial plan is going to allow you to achieve your personal goals, then it will help you maintain the excitement and vision you have for your life. This knowledge will help keep up the momentum during tough times or difficult circumstances when you are making sacrifices.

Budgeting should be the first part of your financial plan, because it will show the money you have coming in and going out. Once you understand your cash flow, then you have all the information you need to make a sound financial plan. Your budget will allow you to make good choices about how you want to use your money and where you can make changes in your spending habits to align your personal goals with your financial goals.

As part of that budgeting process, you need to look at the choices you make on a daily basis. Consider that if you take out that Tinder date on Saturday night maybe you can't afford to play golf on Sunday. If you really want to golf, then maybe you have to Netflix and chill with $1 bottles of beer or a $7 bottle of wine and takeout pizza instead of your dinner and a movie date. We all have to make choices. Just make sure your choices are good choices. You may find that you are sabotaging yourself by the financial decisions you make every day.

The good news is that you don't have to try to figure out a budget on your own or hire a professional to do it for you. All you need is that device that sometimes acts as another appendage – your cell phone. Yes, there is another reason that your cell phone is your best friend because there's an app for that (for budgeting, that is). Actually, there are several apps for that, you just have to choose the one that works best for you.

I use Mint to track my personal bank accounts, credit cards, investments and bills – it creates a budget based on my income and expenses and reminds me when I have a payment due date. I love that my whole financial life is accessible in one place and that I can monitor activity at a glance. One of my daughters uses Clarity Money, which has similar features plus the added benefit of helping to cancel unwanted subscriptions. With an app, you won't have to wonder if you are spending too much money shopping or eating out, you can see it in full color. Knowledge is power, and this knowledge can be used to change your spending behavior to match your financial goals.

For instance, think about that $5 cup of coffee you stop to buy every morning to start your day. That money falls into the sunk costs pot, because you are not getting that money back and it is not working for you. Imagine how much money you could save if you took that $5 per day for a year and saved or invested it – you would have more than $1,825. Going back to those two daughters of mine, one likes to buy and play internet games, a lot – can you guess which one? I'll tell you it's not the one that uses Clarity Money. If you are having trouble saving to meet your long-term goals, then it might be worth exploring using an app to help you get control of your spending.

It is not about giving up your lifestyle, but making your lifestyle adhere to your financial priorities, instead of letting your lifestyle dictate your priorities. Everyone has time to know their money.

Part of achieving any financial goal is to create a nest egg of funds to work with, which serves as a basis for your investment portfolio. Using your budget, you can designate a specific percentage to go into your savings.

STEP 2 – SAVING

The point of saving is to create a financial resource that you can use to build your income streams. These income streams can be diversified, but the point is that saving has to be a priority in order to improve your financial situation and allow you to reach your goals. Here are just a few reasons why saving is important.

1. You have a nest egg for emergencies. Time and time again, financial emergencies have sunk individuals who appear to be doing well, simply because they had nothing to fall back on. Once it happens, they have a financial issue, one that can have a ripple effect across other areas of their lives. Point blank, having an emergency, such as an unexpected car repair or house repair, should not financially sink you. Experts recommend that your savings for emergency needs to cover six months of your living expenses. Once you reach that goal, keep saving a set amount to grow your emergency fund. If you have to use some of it for an emergency, then replace it as soon as possible.

2. You can save for larger purchases. You know that paying cash for items can save you money in the long run, because you won't pay interest on top of the purchase cost. When you designate savings for specific

purchases, it allows you to reach your financial goals without acquiring payments. Plus, once you make that big purchase, you can start saving for the next big item or event.

3. You can save to invest to build income streams. Once you have achieved your emergency savings goal, start building a savings that is specifically for investments. These funds should not be used for any other purpose, allowing you to adjust the rate of return to meet your goals.

Clearly, saving is important because it gives you a stepping stone to meet your financial needs and personal dreams. Now, I want to transition to the exploring the possibilities that you can create with a savings that was started for investing.

STEP 3 – INVESTING

When you reach the point that you have started an investment savings account, you have plenty of opportunities. From stocks and bonds to direct investing in a business, you have multiple ways to grow your investment dollars. That being said, it is important to choose investments that fall in line with your goals and your risk tolerance level.

For instance, if you are at the beginning of your career, you might find yourself more inclined to look for high return, risky investments. Why? Many of those who are younger see time on their side and recognize that they have time to recover from a loss. Alternately, as you reach specific benchmarks or get closer to achieving your financial goals, you will start to make less risky investments.

Another potential scenario is that you are planning to get married or start a family, in which case, you might be more concerned with the risk of losing the primary financial provider. In a case like this, you may be more interested in investing in a disability or life insurance policy or even starting a college fund. After all, not all investments are created equal.

Where you are in your life can play a large part in what type of investments you choose to take on. Additionally, you might take on investments that are less time-consuming because they give you the ability to do more of what you enjoy. On the other hand, you might want to be more hands-on in your investments, so that may be a factor in the types of investments you choose.

Your investment plan should be personalized to you and designed to meet your needs. I want you to recognize that working with a financial advisor can help you to determine the best investments for you.

Many of the individuals I work with even consider investing in themselves, which means starting their own business. If you want to explore your entrepreneurial spirit, that can be a great way to invest and see your returns grow, using your investment dollars and sweat equity. Again, I encourage you to put any investment up against your financial plan. Ask yourself the hard questions about whether it will work towards accomplishing your goals. Doing so is critical to keeping you focused and on the path to achieving both your financial and personal goals. Just keep in mind that it takes time to grow and any time frames set by you can be changed, especially if the situation changes.

STEP 4 – AVOIDING MOST KINDS OF DEBT

Debt can drown you financially and make it difficult for you to achieve your financial goals. When you look at your budget, do you see areas where you are spending money on payments regularly? That is money which is not being used to create income streams or to reach your financial goals.

Be picky when you are choosing to take on debt. I recommend that you only finance things that will bring in money or pay for themselves. It's okay to finance your education because you expect your education to yield you a higher paying career. Do not finance your vacation because you will have nothing but memories to show for it. You can pay for your business advertising with a credit card but not your groceries. Avoid running up your credit cards, leaving yourself strapped with payments. The interest payments can quickly exceed your budget and be a drain. Use the cash in your bank account to pay for your living expenses because the interest on credit cards is usually greater than the interest you earn on money deposited in the bank.

Some debt can be beneficial and preferable because it shares the risk. I am talking about debt that involves investing. For instance, if you are building a real estate portfolio of rentals and you have $100,000 to invest, you might find that you choose to split that $100,000 into down payments for five properties instead of just buying one for $100,000. The reason is that you can increase your cash flow across five properties and they can also cover their own overhead. In the meantime, you are creating equity that you can tap into later to purchase more properties. The point is that you want to use your investment cash to maximize your income opportunities. Do not limit yourself because you want to avoid all debt – some debt can be good.

When weighing your debt options, be sure to look at interest rates. Do not feel as if you are limited to one lender or one financing option. Shop around and make sure that you get the lowest possible rate for your debt with the best payment plan to meet your investment needs. Also, make sure that any investment purchased with debt is going to have a positive cash flow. Some investments may not have a positive cash flow initially but will overtime as the debt is paid down. For other investments, it is the value which grows over time that offsets the lack of a positive cash flow.

Again, it is important to work with a professional who can help you determine what types of debt you want to take on regarding your investments and what debt you want to avoid.

In the end, this step is mostly focused on helping you to avoid debt that drains you financially, without giving you any type of return. Think about the cost of those daily coffees. The focus of this step needs to be on defining the lifestyle you want and then investing in order to be able to afford it. If you opt to live a lifestyle that drains your investments, you could be shortchanging yourself for the future, thus limiting your ability to reach your dreams.

STEP 5 – EVALUATE AND ASSESS: ONGOING PROCESS

I call this step, "the shit happens" part of your plan. Yes, it would be nice if life happened exactly as we planned it, but real life is no fairy tale. The reality is that you made a plan based on the life you wanted to live and all the messy stuff that got in your way is why you had contingency plans, emergency funds and cushions built into your plan. Shit happens, and you deal. You deal by adapting to your new situation. Update your plan as if it is a living, breathing organism.

For instance, you had an accident that kept you from working for six months. That would be both physically and financially draining. This is only a temporary setback. Now you need to reset your goals to achieve your plans, because you may need to focus on rebuilding instead of growth. Still, the point is to make adjustments that help you achieve your goals, thus not allowing the circumstances to overwhelm you and derail your finances permanently.

This need to make adjustments also applies to your investments. I recommend at least once per quarter that you review your investments to make sure they are performing as expected. You don't want to waste your resources on underperforming investments.

Are there areas you might want to expand even further, or do you need to eliminate some investments because they no longer fit your financial goals? Doing these reviews regularly can help you to keep your financial life on track with your personal life. When the two are in sync, then you will find that your life continues to improve. This harmony makes it possible to achieve what you want, no matter the setbacks you might occasionally encounter.

Keep in mind that evaluating and assessing will always be ongoing processes. The fluidity of life is that you can create plans, but events may alter those plans or even offer you new opportunities and experiences that you might not have even considered.

It is important to keep your mind open, both to new investments and to new experiences and opportunities in your personal life. They often can dovetail together more than you ever realize.

Financially, your world is built on the decisions that you make throughout your life. Always know the direction you want to go before you start your journey. When you make decisions without direction, your life will be like a boat without a rudder. It goes all over but doesn't actually get anywhere. The waves take the boat in multiple directions without a clear destination.

I want you to define your path and then work in harmony with that by making choices to complement it. Even with a defined path, it can be easy to make decisions that run contrary to your goals, as I discussed earlier in this chapter. When I work with individuals, I help them to not only define their path, but also to determine the types of goals that align with their paths. Then, I can help them to find the right investments and set financial goals to help them go further on that path.

Growth happens by learning from those people who inspire you to do and be more. We all have time to learn and grow.

Please email Ursula Garrett at ugarrett@cpagarrett.com or visit her website www.cpagarrett.com

Unstoppable

The Art of Striving

DEREK G. CHAN

HOW TO BE UNSTOPPABLE

It has been said that in order to obtain a goal, one must first see it in the mind. The child who decides he wants a cookie from the jar that's high up on the shelf or the person who wants to make partner in the law firm where they now work—each uses the same mechanism or mindset. They understand at a visceral level that you become what you think about.

The difference between the student who can break boards with their hands and feet and the one who can't, isn't skill—it's all mindset, the belief, the deep-seated knowledge that one can do it.

Golf is an interesting game. The person who can best remember the components of a good swing AND can also envision them is the one who will hit the ball far and true and straight. So it is with martial arts: you must develop a set of beliefs or a mindset that will allow you to become unstoppable. Your approach needs to be holistic in nature.

Definition of Holistic: relating to or concerned with wholes or with complete systems rather than with the analysis of, treatment of, or dissection into parts

- Holistic medicine attempts to treat both the mind and the body
- Holistic ecology views humans and the environment as a single system

At Ko Fung Martial Art, we train body, mind and soul, integrating the three elements into a holistic mindset that will make you unstoppable in life.

One of my students, Lesia Rogers, had this to say about our "wellness" approach:

Sifu Derek has truly been a blessing to me, and I am extremely grateful. It has been a year this month since he took me under his wing to teach me how first to love myself. I've also been given many tools through martial art training, coaching and nutrition.

When I first started with Derek, I was already training with someone in Tai Chi, but I'd always wanted to learn self-defence and was looking for a different martial art. Interestingly, the first thing Derek coached me to do was slow down, something I still struggle with to this day.

In the beginning, I was extremely scared and hesitant, but Derek maintained a strong awareness and was always sensitive to my needs. This was important to me as I am an emotional person and needed to reset my mindset to love, acceptance, trust, building confidence and not being afraid of life. He spent hours with me and was by my side through the thick and thin of my life (my accomplishments and my challenges). It has not been an easy journey.

I learned that it takes time for change to happen, that it requires belief in ourselves, and through coaching and training Derek has given me the beautiful gift of awareness of who I really am and what I really want in life. He's made me realize anything is possible if I truly want it. For example, I spent five years with other trainers struggling with little change in my WEIGHT. The first thing Derek did was teach me about mindset to help me understand what it takes to achieve my weight loss goal. By slowing down, listening, AND DOING, I was able to lose 10 pounds in less than two months.

Most recently he has taught me that we often face challenges in life that we have no control over. With the sudden loss of my husband, he has taught me by being there for me that life must go on. In fact, if it wasn't for Derek in the past year, I wouldn't have been prepared to deal with this sudden loss and the corresponding changes in my life.

Change is very scary and can happen suddenly. Although nobody is ever really prepared for tragedy, we must move on and take back control of our lives. Derek has been very supportive and has taught me about acceptance, redirecting and letting go with everything we do in life.

I am a stronger person than I was a year ago when we first started. Thank you to Derek. I know I would be worse off without his coaching.

I had no idea how disciplined martial art can be until I met Derek and learned his way of life. And even though I am now alone (we are never really alone), I am beginning to fill the empty space within by learning to be by myself and love myself truly.

Grateful for every moment and every breath I take, thank you, Sifu Derek.

As mentioned, martial arts represent a pathway to developing a mindset that allows you to be unstoppable. I'll provide a holistic approach to developing this mindset in your own life and give you the tools to deal with hard times whenever you encounter them. You'll learn about martial arts principles and how to apply them to your daily living. Being unstoppable is not about fearlessness or strength, but about recognizing fear and still moving forward.

In training, a martial artist gets used to regular defeats and, in turn, sees them as an opportunity to learn. Tou Lou (martial art routine) or the forms in martial arts teaches us progression. One sequence of movements leads to another. You must learn each fundamental movement first before you can move to the next sequence of movements. This structured type of learning and milestone-based achievement is valuable in all aspects of life.

Wing Chun, in particular, is an effective tool to prepare those who practice it for real life. It does so by developing skills necessary for when one encounters difficult situations. Its concepts and principles are particularly enlightening when properly interpreted and digested under a good Sifu's guidance. Form in the Wing Chun system teaches the practitioner—Awareness, Body Structure, Balance, Body Mechanics and Relaxation. Technique drills or single drills in the Wing Chun system teach the individual how to use those principles during a confrontation.

An essential aspect of having an unstoppable mindset is the ability to make timely decisions in stressful and ambiguous situations. A decision may be either right or wrong, but it's crucial to remember that far worse than an incorrect decision is a situation where no decision is made when one is necessary. Through a variety of cooperative and semi-cooperative drills, a Wing Chun practitioner is able to develop intuition, reflexes and decision-making skills while under pressure.

An example of a Wing Chun drill that develops these skills is the famous 'Chi Sao' (sticking hand) training. It is a two-person tactile sensitivity drill. One only does the attacking while the other is only defending. The objective of the attacker is learning how to use leverage, distance, angle and openings to create a successful attack. At the same time, the defender is learning how to maintain proper body structure, relaxation and counter movements while under pressure with unplanned attacks. The key to Chi Sao is accepting the force coming in (relaxation) instead of using force against force.

This develops decision-making skills through checking assumptions against facts, and develops problem-solving by making its practitioners consider the possible impact of their decisions throughout the process of the drill. This gives the two practitioners an opportunity to test their strengths and weakness while promoting unique and unplanned learning processes to occur.

POWER OF BREATH - STRESS MANAGEMENT

A crucial concept in Wing Chun is that of proper breathing. Siu Nim Tao is the first open hand form from the Wing Chun system and is a form of breathing meditation. Siu Nim Tao translates to "Little Idea," meaning everything starts with a thought. Without proper breathing, movement becomes stilted and ineffective. Proper abdominal breathing is a skill that is crucial for a healthier and stronger body and also for focus, which is why it is one of the first things taught.

In addition to the health and training benefits of breathing, it can also be used as an important tool for stress management. Breathing has both voluntary and involuntary control mechanisms. You can shift from being its pilot to allowing it to be left on autopilot. The voluntary aspect of breathing is what allows us to tap into its stress-managing potential.

Breathing exercises act as a form of meditation in Chinese Martial Arts. Proper abdominal breathing used in this type of meditation allows a greater volume of breath and leads to a decrease in activity of stress markers and blood levels of stress hormones.

Oftentimes, when our life is stressed, the integrity of our automatic breathing suffers. Taking advantage of the control we can exert on breathing allows us to combat stress. Learning to control our breathing can allow us to begin to control other parts of our body as well. The mind-body connection developed through breathing exercises not only physically improves our breathing but can also increase self-awareness. When you bring your body and mind in tune, your mental state will be much improved, and less susceptible to stress.

BODY STRUCTURE

Martial arts teach the skills of how to use your body structure to your advantage, and offers understanding on how the body's structure works in terms of structural alignment, the linkage of the joints, and also how simple geometry and physics can be applied to the body. A central focus of Wing Chun is adopting particular stances and postures as a framework from which to launch attacks and counter-attacks. Doing this without good posture will greatly limit your ability to be effective. In fact, your Wing Chun techniques won't be as effective unless your body is aligned correctly. This alignment also reinforces the important concept of breathing and can directly impact your ability to draw and use your breath.

Good posture means that the body is aligned with gravity, walks tall and moves with freedom in the joints. Posture in martial arts is vitally important.

This is the reason most martial arts emphasize structure from the beginning. Physical structure from a Kung Fu point of view involves a little more than just good posture, though. In addition to good posture, it adds internal connections such that your entire body learns to move as a single fluid and powerful unit.

The efficient way to get a feel for a student's structure is through single drills, Chi Sao and sparring. Good structure can be almost invisible—even to the trained eye. However, the lack of it can usually be felt as soon as contact is made with your opponent. If an opponent has good structure, a lot of techniques you could try are unlikely to work, but if their structure is poor or non-existent, almost anything you do will be effective.

What exactly is good structure and why is it so important? To put it in simple terms, good structure is the way in which you connect the different parts of yourself together internally so that they are aligned with the forces acting on your body. In Wing Chun principle and theory, the curves of the spine should be aligned, eliminating as much curvature as much as possible. It's done by tucking in the chin backward and slightly scooping forward the tailbone to avoid an anterior pelvic title. Shoulders should be relaxed and dropping with the body. By doing so, the body is able to absorb and deliver a force as one bodily unit.

The majority of people are completely disconnected and don't have proper alignment and coordination with their body. Their arms will do one thing, their legs something different, with hips only being vaguely involved. When the body does so many different things, it's impossible to connect the breath or the mind to what it's doing. This results in internal chaos and a feeling that you lack the resources to cope with your physical situation. The truth is, you don't lack the resources at all; you've just scattered them. The key to good structure is in learning how to gather all the parts of yourself together so that you can put everything you are into everything you do.

Good structure connects your arms and legs together through your centre and involves your breath working in harmony with your movements. Most important, the whole process is controlled by your mind, which stays focused on what you're doing. When you're connected internally, every movement involves your whole body. This internal structure can easily be felt. For example, when you try to move someone's arm who is well connected internally, you can feel that in trying to move their arm you are moving the weight of their whole body.

RELAXATION

Relaxation is a great example taught in martial arts that can easily be applied to everyday life. To be relaxed is to be natural. It should be like pouring water into your cup without any muscle tension. To get a better understanding of how to apply this in daily life, we remember how relaxation, in the context of martial arts, is supposed to be understood.

When I teach Wing Chun, I like to begin by emphasizing to my students that, in training, techniques are performed in a relaxed manner. This occurs both during training and in actual combat. In order to develop force, one must be able to relax. Why? The equation for force is mass times acceleration, and if there's any sort of muscle tension, it will only slow down the acceleration. I tend to use an analogy of a car. In order for a car to move smoothly, you will have to step on the accelerator. Step on the brake and accelerator at the same time, and it will feel like you're getting a lot of power, but in reality, you're not going anywhere.

If the arm is tensed, maximum punching speed cannot be achieved. To begin a punch motion, the arm must, in essence, be first relaxed. If relaxed at the onset, the punch may begin at any time. It is a fact that one motion is always faster than two. If there is unnecessary tension, energy will be wasted, and this will, in turn, create fatigue. In an extended engagement, this can be critical. Tension stiffens your body and thus reduces your ability to sense and react to your opponent's intentions. Look at the sport of boxing. The best boxers don't get tired—even after 12 rounds. A huge part of this is that they don't waste energy on inefficient movement. Less experienced boxers may look good early in a fight, but they often crumble in the later rounds due to not being relaxed.

I will now paraphrase two of the core points of this lesson:

1. **Tense muscle slows down your reaction speed.**
2. **Unnecessary tension wastes energy, causing fatigue.**

If you're overcome by anger or are tense, your mind faces identical effects and, consequently, you'll have difficulty acting with the speed you need. This unnecessary tension in your mind doesn't only waste your energy and time, it also creates a lot of undesired situations that will now need to be solved. A person with a relaxed mind can always see things more clearly than a quick-tempered person. Thus, they can easily react with proper speed and attitude. This is why a person who understands the principle of relaxation correctly can certainly be more careful and successful; they react only when necessary by keeping calm and relaxed.

BALANCE

Balance is important to all martial arts, and especially Wing Chun. It's a concept that ties together both relaxation and structure. Without balance you can't maintain structure, nor can you be relaxed as you'll always be fighting to right yourself and the structure you've moved away from.

The Merriam-Webster dictionary defines balance as follows:

bal·ance noun \ba-lən(t)s
- The state of having your weight spread equally so that you do not fall
- The ability to move or to remain in a position without losing control or falling
- A state in which different things occur in equal or proper amounts or have an equal or proper amount of importance

Balance in Kung Fu is often associated with the physical sense of the word. I teach my students from the day they walk in how to understand their bodies in order to develop the balance necessary to perform the forms and techniques in Wing Chun. However, physical isn't the only form of balance a martial arts student should learn to hone. Balance in Wing Chun isn't only about your own physical body, but understanding how to create balance between two individuals. The highest level in the art of Wing Chun isn't about how to destroy or how to inflict the most pain in an individual, but how to neutralize and balance an opponent's incoming force without harming them, and at the same time preventing them from hurting you.

> *"The best battle is the one that has not been fought."*
> - Sun Tzu

This is one of the other reasons why in Wing Chun we'll focus heavily on

Chi Sao, as it understands how to find balance between two individuals—either by changing to a different position or stepping in a different angle. This is one of the skills that's transferable to everyday life and relationship-building.

There is a saying that Wing Chun Kung Fu is easy to learn but hard to master. One reason is that, in the Wing Chun system, there's a fine balance between each movement and technique. Each movement needs to be precise. There can't be any gray area as it could be a matter of your life or death in a physical confrontation. In order to find the fine balance, though, one must understand not what to do but what not to do.

Understanding this concept will also help you find balance with your overall well-being and health. It's not about knowing what type of workout we should be doing or what type of food we should eat, but what we should not be doing or eating on a daily basis. Example: all rigorous physical activity can wear down the body, and you can feel tired, sore or injured. One must always balance training and rest, and in the case of an injury, you must listen to your body. Training when too fatigued or coming back too soon from an injury can set your training back by keeping you out even more in the long run.

ROOTING AND CENTRALIZATION

"When you have roots there is no reason to fear the wind."
- Chinese Proverb

In order to understand how to become unstoppable in classical martial arts training you must recognize that it all begins with the foundation. So what does the foundation include? Strengthening the lower body by lowering your center of gravity and widening up your base. Learning how to align your skeletal structure at the same time as relaxing your body. If we're able to be rooted to the ground and our body is up straight, it's most likely going to be harder to be pushed out of balance. You can try this when you are taking the bus or subway.

1. Imagine your head is being slightly pulled up.

2. Widen your base (knees are a shoulder width apart).

3. Slightly bend your knees to lower your center of gravity.

You'll automatically feel more balanced and centered. A solid base is required in order for you to grow your skills and techniques. It's the same in life. It's important to understand what keeps you grounded, to discover both your values and your beliefs. By doing so, you're able to hold your ground no matter what conditions life gives you.

By being grounded, you'll eliminate fear and find inner peace. This happens as you gain the courage and strength to overcome whatever fears you might have. Training in the martial arts will always push you to your limits. It tests not only your physical strength but your mental strength as well. Know this: each time you're ready to give up, you're facing a true test of willpower. You push yourself to the limit to see how much more you can take and to see how much more you're willing to go through in order to achieve your goal. This mental strength develops into an unbreakable warrior spirit, giving you the courage to persevere through your darkest hours.

ACCEPTANCE AND LETTING GO

At a certain point in your training the ability to 'let go' becomes essential. The concept of letting go functions on two levels—physical and mental. To be able to truly let go, the physical, mental (includes emotional) aspects must function in unison.

Physically you learn to relax and release your muscles, tendons and ligaments. When you do this, it leads to the deepening of one's root and the ability to ground a powerful incoming force. In terms of meditation, this means relaxing as much as possible and 'trusting' the Earth to hold you up.

The emotional and mental aspects of 'letting go' are intertwined, meaning that emotions can trigger thought patterns, and certain thought patterns can trigger emotions. You should look for evenness and balance in your emotion. This is a non-reactive state rather than an absence of emotion per se. This emotional neutrality is like a placid lake that appears to be a mirror. In this state, it becomes possible to read a person's true emotional intention like an open book.

For the mind, you want, at first, a gentle calmness and a slowing of thought, but this eventually develops into what has been termed 'mind of no mind.' This mind of no mind is actually an optimal state for both the meditative aspect as well as the martial. For meditation, we can perceive and become aware of things without the mind's judgement. In martial arts, this 'mind of no mind' state is optimal for success in combat. When centered in such a state you are able to act or react at a speed that can be faster than the speed of thought!

Accepting and letting go are probably two of the hardest things to do. Whether it's a relationship, anger from an argument or simply past mistakes: instead of being stuck in the moment, accept the emotion and the situation with your arms wide open. Acknowledge, embrace and let go. Let go of emotions and situations that don't serve you as a whole or lead you to greater things. It's beyond whether you were right or wrong. It's about setting yourself free. It begins with the willingness to accept ourselves exactly as we are, right where we are, with no judgements or preconceived notions. For the martial element, you must go even further. Instead of fearing an opponent's attack, you must learn to welcome it. This is all a matter of lack of tension. Therefore, the stronger an attack, the more relaxed you must initially become to deal with it. This method is grounded in a Wing Chun principle that states, "Accept what comes, escort what leaves." By accepting the incoming force, it will enable you to reposition and let go of what's coming in at you.

Once this is accomplished you no longer react to circumstances as average people do. Instead, you find yourself centered and alert—ready to deal with a situation without having your natural adrenal reaction getting in the way. This is not only supremely useful in combat but also in your daily life.

MOVING FORWARD

"Your one-step back is your opponent's two-step forward."
–Derek G. Chan

One of the most important rules of Wing Chun is that you don't step back. It is structure that gives us the advantage over the larger opponent, and when we become our worst enemy by destroying our own structure, it's not too difficult to predict the outcome of a fight. While Wing Chun may have backward stepping and backward bracing, these footworks are not designed for you to initiate. In Wing Chun we always move forward; only when the force dictates it do we actually move backwards. Footwork in Wing Chun is always taking you forward. It might be in a direct straight line or at an angle, but it allows you to swallow up any space that opens up between you and an attacker, limiting their options and overwhelming them.

Some of the most skilful boxers are those that can deliver a knockout blow while going backwards. While this may be much to the appreciation of the crowd, Wing Chun has no time for any of this. The footwork drives you forward all the time. One of the most important rules I always remind my students of during our sparring sessions is to continue to move forward—mentally and physically. It's important to create opportunities either by footwork, by stepping in a different angle, or a follow-up technique. There may be times when it is best to be stationary and wait for the perfect timing and openings. However, if you are against a more experienced opponent, the only chance of you overcoming the situation is by closing the distance and creating the opening. If you don't, not only do you have a lesser chance of winning, you're also leaving yourself vulnerable as a stationary target.

By having the attitude of forward movement, it will greatly benefit you in your daily life. Life is your experienced and stronger opponent. It doesn't matter how organized or how well-planned you are; life will always throw obstacles at you. In order for you to conquer them, you must start by moving forward. If you keep waiting for the perfect time or the perfect day, you'll never get anything done, and, sadly, you'll also miss a lot of opportunities. Instead, start moving forward and create your own path, regardless of how tough the situation is. If there's a will there is a way.

FOCUS

It can take a continuous daily effort to reach your goals. However, focusing on your long-term expectations, you'll find the strength to keep going even in the face of temporary setbacks. Those trained in Wing Chun will tell you that in the process you'll face a lot of challenges and setbacks. The students who are able to recognize that such setbacks are necessary hurdles and pitfalls they must navigate along the path to their destination are also the ones who succeed. Without that realization a student faces great difficulty overcoming those setbacks because they may lose sight of their long-term goals and allow themselves to get lost, joining the many casualties who fall by the wayside.

To focus, you must not only find a goal but also envision and look beyond at what lies ahead. The same principle applies to Karate practitioners when they attempt to break boards. If they only focus on the surface, their success rate of breaking the boards decreases as their force will be slowed down before they reach the target. However, if they are envisioning and telling themselves to hit behind or through the boards, the chance of them breaking the board is a lot higher.

Life is a series of experiences. There will be times where you're stuck in the moment. Whether it's a failure in a business partnership or the loss of a family member, it's up to you to endure and envision what lies ahead and continue to march forward. By doing so, you'll develop a stronger self and character. This is what separates those who are short-sighted from those who are long-sighted.

TECHNIQUE—EFFICIENCY AND ECONOMICAL

"Offence is Defence, Defence is Offence."
- Wing Chun Proverb

One of Wing Chun's unique points is that it doesn't rely on any brute strength to overcome an adversary. We'll always place ourselves as the fragile person. Why? There will always be someone bigger, stronger and faster. And the way to overcome a larger assailant is by understanding the power of proper body structure and relaxation.

To become more efficient and economical with your movements, you'll defend and attack simultaneously. Doing so will allow you to become more efficient with your movements. One example is the Lap Da or Lap

Sao technique. This is a technique where one hand sinks the opponent's straight attack while your other hand punches. In order to execute these fine movements, there will be an emphasis on body coordination drills. Without being coordinated, you wouldn't have the ability to execute the technique as smoothly. Wing Chun techniques often require you to have your hands and lower body cooperating with one another. Being well coordinated also means one is well-balanced. As human beings, we already apply the principle of balance while we are walking. Our left hand will swing out. Right foot steps forward, and vice versa. However, as a martial artist sometimes we tend to forget about this basic principle, and we think martial arts movements and everyday movements are two separate entities.

Having the Wing Chun mindset of being efficient will change our approach to handling daily tasks. It will help us realize how important it is to utilize our energy more efficiently (as it will help us manage time). In Wing Chun philosophy, time is an important factor. For this reason, each movement and technique has to be precise. As it could be a matter of life or death if you're in a confrontation. Every inch, every angle, every movement comes into play. Wing Chun is a system that does not discriminate, as it is not about who is bigger, stronger and faster. It's about understanding how to utilize proper body mechanics and physics to your advantage. It's understanding how to execute the most impactful thing efficiently and effectively in the limited time and energy you're given. This is why, in classical martial arts, you'll strike on vital spots and soft tissues on the opponent when placed in a life or death situation. By embracing this Wing Chun concept, you're able to focus more and utilize your time and energy more efficiently and effectively in your regular daily routine.

To learn more about Derek's method of Wing Chun visit us at
www.kofung.ca or contact us at info@kofung.ca

Achieving a Better Legacy for Private Music Students

STEPHEN RICHES

Have you reached a point in your life where you would like to try a new activity or learn a new skill? Why haven't you? If you are like many people, a few failed attempts make you believe that you aren't talented enough to master the skill set, or perhaps you believe you are too old to start. The process gets abandoned and you chalk it up to something that "wasn't meant to be."

The reality is that this does not need to happen. Becoming talented is neither a mysterious nor a daunting process, but rather, like most things in life, simply one that requires a proven successful plan of action. So right now would be a great time for you to change your perception of your own ability.

In my first book, Talent CAN Be Taught: The Book on Creating Music Ability, I debunked the myth that music talent or skill is something that only a few of the elite may enjoy, and introduced the acronym, PRAISE™, which will provide you and students everywhere with an actual blueprint for successfully developing your music skills. Even better, many of these principles may be applied in other areas of your life.

Your ability to achieve can often be wrapped up in how you view yourself. Do you see your skills as the assets that they are, or do you find yourself setting up barriers to your own success? And, with the recent discoveries by neuroscientists that point to the fact that by developing music skills you also greatly improve your brain structure and function, there may be no better way to equip yourself for a lifetime than to invest in yourself with music training.

In this chapter, I will introduce to you the principles that I have used to help my students grow music talent. Some of these, undoubtedly, will seem very logical and straightforward to you. So, if you have ever dreamed of having music talent, don't allow your fears of what others might think to stand in your way. The first step, especially if you ever had lessons in the past but gave up on your dream, is to understand that the reason most students lose interest, become discouraged and quit is because the system failed to ensure that they received the basic training that they needed to succeed.

In fact, private music lessons have presented insurmountable challenges for almost all beginning students for many decades. The problems that arise are the result of the strategies used by most music teachers and teaching studios, rather than with the students themselves, who, unfortunately, are usually blamed for their own lack of success. And, the root cause of the entire problem is one that stems from a general misunderstanding about what talent really is and how talent is created in the first place. So that is where I start my chapter.

UNDERSTANDING TALENT

Many people consider talent to be something that is innate; something that you either have or do not have, and over which you have no control. This is, in large part, due to the ideas that most of us have regarding what talent really is. If we see someone who is very young who displays music ability, we tend to say that this person is very talented. But this begs the question that if someone who is older has developed the very same skills, why should this older person not be considered to be equally talented.

In other words, why should talent simply be considered the domain of those who learn more quickly or at a younger age? Should talent not be evaluated on the basis of skills that can be demonstrated, rather than the age or the speed at which they were acquired? Just as "the proof of the pudding is in the eating", so the evidence of the talent is in the performing, rather than the age of the performer. It is these special music skills or abilities that set talented people apart and which are an indicator of their talent.

A FAILING TRADITION

Whether or not talent can be acquired is something that has been debated for many years. But where there is certainly no doubt is that in the vast majority of cases, beginning students do not become talented. And it is perhaps this fact that has led so many people to assume that their failure to progress well in developing music skills was due to an innate lack of pre-existing talent in the first place. The truth, however, is that millions of people have been victims of a failing tradition in private music education. In my book, Talent CAN Be Taught™, I first identify the signs of this systemic failure, and then present strategies that are providing exciting solutions for my students. This chapter highlights a few of the main points.

The reality is that well over 90% of all students quit private music lessons within a couple of months to a few years and go through the rest of their lives unable to perform any of the pieces that they ever learned, believing that they were responsible for their own lack of success. The causes of this high failure rate rest with critical mistakes and teaching strategies made especially by parents and teachers.

I refer to one of the causes of this failing tradition as the Tom Sawyer School of Learning, after the character in the Mark Twain novel who is able to present documented evidence of achievement without actually ever having done the required work, or acquiring the knowledge that his evidence suggests he has. First of all, he devises a strategy to get paid by his friends so that they can have the privilege of doing the work of whitewashing his aunt's fence, which she had intended to be a punishment for him skipping school the day before. And then he buys Sunday school tickets from his friends the next day by selling their loot back to them in order to receive an honour which he has not earned, in the form of an award given to all those who manage to memorize two thousand Bible verses. In the end, however, the fraud is exposed in front of the entire community, as he is unable to even correctly identify the names of just two of Jesus' disciples.

It is an unfortunate fact, however, that parents, students, and teachers sometimes work together in a way that actually defeats the system, in the same manner as Mark Twain's fictional character does. Due to a quest by parents and students to achieve accreditation as quickly as possible, teachers fail to help students to acquire any of the actual music skills that are the real purpose of the lessons in the first place. Parents and students engage in as few lessons as possible. Teachers skip pages of the curriculum books, books of curriculum levels, entire levels of curricula, and in general then "hopscotch" their way through RCM grades to acquire a Grade 7 and/or Grade 8 RCM certificate for high school credits or to pad their resumes for future career opportunities. Some students have learned as few as a couple of dozen pieces over all of their years of private music training to accomplish this feat. They do not actually learn to read music, nor do they develop the ability to play by ear, which are the two most basic of all music skills. Due to the enormous struggle involved in learning advanced level pieces with undeveloped or under-developed reading skills, even students who manage to survive hate this process so much that they abandon the music they learned forever. As a result, there is a great multitude of students who have achieved Grade 8 level of Royal Conservatory of Music certificates who are unable to play even a single piece of music that they have ever learned.

So, to summarize the problem, some of the most obvious signs of this failing tradition are:

- Inability to remember and perform any music that was ever learned

- Inability to read music at sight beyond a very elementary level, sometimes even Pre-Grade 1

- Inability to learn or play new music by ear

- Deficiencies in technical skill development

- Lack of understanding of musical style

- A more than 90% dropout rate of all beginners every three years

Compounding the problem is that many private music teachers themselves have been the product of this failing tradition. In many cases, not only do they not perform publicly themselves, but they don't even perform for their students, despite the fact that this is the most effective of all teaching strategies. Further, despite their own weaknesses, they have no plans for their own personal professional development. And so, predictably, they continue to use the same failing strategies that led to their own weaknesses and duplicate these shortcomings in their own students.

The Powerful PRAISE Techniques™ explained in detail in my first book called Talent CAN Be Taught: The Book on Creating Music Ability are the key steps which form the blueprint for successfully creating music ability. The word PRAISE is an acronym for these six very important steps to success. Following is a brief synopsis of these key steps.

THE 6 POWERFUL PRAISE TECHNIQUES™

Performance & Repertory – The Core Essence of Music
Why the system begins with performance

Music begins with performance because music is a performance art. If music isn't performed by someone, it doesn't exist. A repertory is a personal collection of music that a particular performer can play at any time by memory.

Results & Accreditation – The Benchmarks of Achievement
The value of certificates and goal setting

While seeking to acquire certificates rather than usable music skills is to put the proverbial cart before the horse, accreditation does have a valuable role to play in measuring student progress. Awards and certificates honour achievement and provide goals for the achievement of excellence. These important measurable, attainable, and most importantly, dated goals for achievement are important steps in the learning process, without which all achievement is jeopardized.

Acceleration & Motivation – The MAGIC of Synergy™
The power of this element in the learning process

One of the reasons that so many students give up on themselves is that they perceive that the learning process is taking too long and they lose interest. Most students, due to poor strategies used by their parents and teachers, never are able to develop any synergy of learning. Acquiring momentum, enjoying accelerated learning, experiencing growth of skills and abilities, feeling inspired to become even better, and being motivated by competition, (either internal or external), to achieve as high a standard of excellence as possible, are all very important steps to success for everyone in all aspects of life. Becoming musically talented is no exception.

Insights & Strategies – The Philosophy of Education
"Only perfect practice makes perfect"

Talent CAN Be Taught presents a number of important insights and strategies for the successful development of music skills. For example, it is a common misconception that practice makes perfect. Student failures, in fact, are often blamed either on a lack of talent or a lack of practice, both of which fail to recognize the real cause of the failures. This famous and often mis-quoted Vince Lombardi gem is one example of a philosophy or insight that is presented in the book. What the legendary football coach actually said was that "perfect practice makes perfect". However, the reality is that beginners do not know how to practice, and bad practice never achieves good results. In fact, practicing independently usually leads to frustration for almost all beginners. All students need to be first taught how to practice rather than just what to practice. And students should only be asked to practice after they have been well-prepared for independent learning. This necessarily includes having some basic reading and ear training skills. Most beginners, however, are too young to understand and use sound pedagogical strategies for independent learning. As a result, independent practice often causes more harm than good in the beginning stages of training. In the early stages, practice needs to be monitored by an expert.

Supervision & Curriculum – The Tools of Training
The role of teachers and teaching materials

Private independent teachers, by definition, have no supervisory support. Nor do many follow a curriculum in its entirety to ensure that all concepts are taught. Many or most parents either do not understand or perhaps underestimate the value or importance of the role that supervision and curriculum have to play in a student's training even though it is taken for granted in public education. The music skills that we recognize as indicators of talent do not happen by accident or over time by independent practice alone. Like all skills in all vocations, they must be taught by an expert. An important part of the TCBT system is in making sure that our teachers are equipped to provide the most expert training possible for the students. This philosophy is at the core of all that has led to the great successes of our unique Talent CAN Be Taught™ system.

The most important factor in education for all teachers and students is the need for an outstanding comprehensive and sequential curriculum. Many curricula have weaknesses in the sequence or order that concepts are taught, the size of the challenges presented to the students, and in maintaining consistently small and attainable and progressive steps for learning. These shortcomings always contribute to frustration. However, the TCBT system follows what we consider to be the very best curriculum available, which we mandate to be used by all of our teachers and students. This is also discussed in some detail in the book.

Why is using a good curriculum so important? Well, first of all, teachers are able to follow it as a daybook to systematically track the lessons that they provide. And, students who follow it are able to avoid developing gaps in their music education that always cause the learning experience to become slower, more frustrating, and less enjoyable with every level of advancement. The irony is that the shortcuts that are often taken in the quest for faster advancement and achieving higher certificates at an earlier date actually slow down the learning process. By contrast, with the TCBT system, student skill development is occurring so rapidly that some of the students have progressed from Grade 1 to Grade 6 in only two years without skipping any grade levels or exams, and have achieved First Class Honours on their exams at every level while learning hundreds of pieces of music during that time.

Ear Training & Reading Skills – The Basic Fundamentals
"Do you play by ear, or do you read music?"

As a young person, I often had an opportunity to perform for recitals or other occasions or special events. Invariably, people would see me perform by memory and ask whether I read music or played by ear. My answer, of course, was "both". At the time, I had no idea how profound this response was. For what other method is there? Either you play by ear, or you read music, and ideally both, for these are the two fundamentally basic of all music skills. And yet, both of these important skills are among the common denominators that are missing for the vast majority of students who quit taking lessons after just a few months or years. They quit because they cannot read music, nor can they play by ear, and so they find it frustrating trying to learn mainly by rote and are not enjoying it. The Talent CAN Be Taught™ system ensures that ear and reading skills are actually taught, and these vital and basic fundamentals which are taught at every step of the way complete the six Powerful PRAISE Techniques™ that contribute to the great success of the students.

The Achievers Programs™
The success of the pilot program

The Achievers Programs™ were developed to ensure student success in keeping with the principles outlined in the six Powerful PRAISE Techniques™ that make up the core part of the TCBT system. The inspiration that led to the development of these accelerated learning programs resulted from the experience of one particular student and the strategy that I implemented as a pilot program for him. This student had chosen to begin taking a trial month of guitar lessons. He could not read music, and did not know how to practice, and had become frustrated very quickly trying to practice independently six days a week. Within two weeks, he had lost interest and stopped practicing. So we made a switch. Instead of guitar, we gave him a fresh start on piano. I made a deal with him that he didn't have to practice, in order to eliminate the tension at home that had occurred due to his Mom's insistence that he had to practice every day. We gave him three half-hour lessons per week instead of one, and I reduced the price per lesson as an incentive to invest more overall to the strategy. Of course, we also used the outstanding house piano/keyboard curriculum. There were, and still are today, five main goals of this program as follows:

- provide more frequent, regular, expert teacher support

- reduce per-lesson cost to encourage parents to make a larger short-term financial commitment

- enhance foundational learning with a switch to piano training

- eliminate the source of tension and liabilities associated with forced independent practice

- to create synergy among the various learning components with the frequency of instruction

Less than three months after starting this pilot program, I discovered that the student, who had been working with another teacher at my studio, was beginning the fifth level in the curriculum. And this curriculum had 4 books at each level. His mother had this explanation for how he had managed to go through 16 curriculum books in just 10 weeks:

"Oh, I forgot to tell you. He won't stop practicing. He practices at all hours during the day, even first thing in the morning before school. I put an alarm clock on the piano set for 8:15 AM. I tell him that when the alarm goes off, he has to stop playing the piano and go to school, or he is going to be late. I may be upstairs vacuuming and hear the alarm go off. I turn off the vacuum cleaner to listen, and the sounds from the piano keep on going. So I have to come downstairs to physically remove him from the piano bench and send him off to school."

So what happened here? Well, this student, who had previously very quickly become disinterested in the instrument of his choice (guitar), was now thriving on piano as a result of the implementation of the Powerful PRAISE Techniques™ that form the core principles of the TCBT system. I immediately began to promote these strategies for all of our students. Within three years, all of the students who participated in the program were able to accelerate through as many as eight levels of study achieving excellence at every level.

BUILDING A NEW LEGACY FOR THE FUTURE

An Innovative Teacher Apprentice Program

The best of systems can only reach its ultimate achievement when it is duplicated. That, of course is the principle behind the great successes of franchising. And just as many teachers are duplicating their own weaknesses in their students and thereby contributing to the continuation of the failing traditions, so the TCBT teacher apprentice program has been designed to continue and duplicate a new and better system of private music education. This program is designed especially for high school age students who have achieved RCM First Class Honours in Grade 5 Piano and Basic Theory. Students who have not yet achieved this standard of excellence, but who are currently studying at this level may also be admitted to the program. In the apprentice program, students are provided with an opportunity to first improve the quality of their own learning through examination of teaching practices and study of curriculum materials, to earn community service credits for high school by assisting beginning students, and eventually to earn part-time income through teaching beginning level students themselves. Those who progress to the highest levels of achievement will have an opportunity to become leaders of the Talent CAN Be Taught™ system to continue the legacy for future generations.

While piano/keyboard training is the best foundation for all music studies, the principles, of course, are transferable to other instruments and voice. At TCBT studios, we encourage many students to diversify and take a second instrument when they are ready for the additional experience. Some may receive this supplemental training in the public education system, but many do not. And all benefit greatly from receiving supplemental expert support with their band or orchestra instrument that isn't available in the context of a music classroom setting. Without exception, these students become the leaders in their school music programs.

AN AFTERWORD TO THE CHAPTER

In Talent CAN Be Taught; The Book on Creating Music Ability, I drew attention to the shortcuts that students were taking, and the resulting mine field that causes almost all private music students to get frustrated and give up on themselves within a few months to a few years. They incorrectly assumed, or in some cases were perhaps even told that the reason that they were not progressing was because they lacked talent, when, in fact, the real reason was due to historically ineffective teaching routines and strategies, and especially the ill-advised shortcuts that have been used by parents, teachers, and students for many years. These are explained in detail in the book, along with numerous recommended solutions.

In this single chapter, therefore, I have merely summarized and highlighted some of the key points of the book, while necessarily leaving out an explanation of most of the important details.

So while I hope that you found this chapter helpful as an introduction to the topic of how to ensure quality results with private music lessons, I encourage anyone who is serious about developing music skills to read the entire book.

In summary, the book includes a detailed explanation of many of the most common errors made by parents, students, and private teachers engaged in private music education. It also includes a diagnostic survey that will help readers to recognize if they have been a victim themselves of what I refer to as the failing traditions. Finally, it provides the proven blueprint for success through a detailed explanation of the role of The Powerful PRAISE Techniques™, as well as a number of helpful insights and strategies for success. These are critically important for all students of any age who would like to have great music skills, even for those who had previously given up on their own personal quest for talent, and who may now be inspired to renew their efforts buoyed by a better understanding of the proven keys to success.

TESTIMONIALS

"Stephen's vision and commitment to achieving a better future for private music education is truly inspiring. His passion for excellence, which I have been privileged to observe firsthand, is evident in his book's reflections and challenge for future engagement."

Reg Andrews
Administrator, Pickering Christian Academy, (Markham, ON)
www.pca.ca

"If your child is now or soon will be taking piano lessons, you need to read this book, because all students deserve to have teachers who really understand and value the important lessons this book contains."

Frank Feather
global business futurist, author, and father to two pianist daughters (Aurora, ON)
www.ffeather.com

"I took piano lessons for 9 years as a child and today, I cannot play anything! I thought that was because I was not naturally talented. If I had understood the concepts in this book – that talent can be taught – today I would be a professional piano player, entertaining people around the world!"

Dr. Robert A. Rohm Ph.D
speaker, author (Atlanta, GA)
www.personalityinsights.com

"I first met Stephen around the time he published his first book. I was so impressed with his commitment to making changes to improve how music is taught for the benefit of students everywhere that I invited him to be co-author of my second volume of *The Road to Success*"

Jack Canfield
entrepreneur, success coach, and co-author of the
Chicken Soup for the Soul books (Santa Barbara, CA)
www.jackcanfield.com

Your Life Energy

AMAL INDI

I have 20 years of experience in the tech sector and corporate banking. In my previous life in the "Rat Race", I was waking up every day and going to a job that provided well for me. After some major changes in my life (including a divorce), I started recognizing that I wasn't intrinsically happy. I would be going about my day filled with negative thoughts and emotions. It felt as though they were taking over in a way, and I recognized how they were beginning to affect every moment of my day and every interaction with those around me. I refer to these as "Thought Bugs", which I will go on to explain later. These Thought Bugs were almost like a computer virus, affecting all the thoughts or, as one may say, programming in my mind. After recognizing these Bugs and studying them in myself for many years, I began to draw strong conclusions about how I could create positive change in my mind. This positive change in my thoughts would eventually lead to me leaving the "Rat Race" and starting on the mission of my life to share my new paradigm with those around me. I believe that we can change our minds and create a positive and uplifting life, not only for ourselves, but for those around us. I would love to share with you the basics of what I discovered, a new way of examining our thought patterns and how to drastically shift the energy around you (your Aura) so that you can lead a fantastic life!

GETTING STARTED ON YOUR OWN JOURNEY

When was the last time you really felt 100%? When I say 100%, I mean you wake up feeling a general positivity in your mood, you are looking forward to a new day, your interactions with people feel good, and you walk around feeling a general sense of purpose even with the simple tasks of getting groceries or whatever your work environment. You may think that you have no say in how you really feel. That deep down, you cannot control your thoughts and emotions. I know that this is not true. I developed a unique way of seeing our minds and how deeply they affect our energy. Have you heard of life energy, such as positive energy, negative energy, Aura energy, and universal energy? Read on!

WHAT MAKES US HUMAN?

Each one of us is a biological marvel of different cells, tissues, genes. These are the many working pieces that come together to create our human body. What really makes us human in a whole sense? We each possess an in-depth energetic landscape that we can't deny. This energetic pulse is used by scientists and technicians daily to perform tests and create pictures of our bodies and their functions. Think of the neuroscientists that connect our bodies to electrodes and measure our brain waves. That's part of it. We can't deny there is a part of us beyond just the tissues of our muscles and bones.

Did you know that surrounding you right now is an energy field that is all your own? This energetic field is referred to as your Aura. This Aura can be the beginning of a life that you love. Every human being has an energy field around them. We cannot see this field with the naked eye. However, we can see this field with an Aura machine. It's true! I personally have had mine captured and what was reflected back to me (in terms of energetic levels) was what I was truly feeling.

Your Aura and the energy you radiate is 100% in your control. Some days, you might feel positive and good, while other days, you may feel more negative and lower. These are your energy levels. They can vibrate high or low. It depends on you and your thoughts. Remember, with improvements to your mind and thoughts, your aura energy field will continuously change, thus altering the life you are leading.

YOUR AURA

Over the centuries of humans existing and contemplating our existence, many have acknowledged the fact that we have an energy that extends beyond our skin and flesh, which can actually interact with the world around us. This is referred to as your body's Aura. The Aura refers to the energy around your body that can be affected from the inside out or the outside in. When it is strong, the Aura around your body can extend quite a way beyond the barrier of your physical body (your skin). It can also manifest as different colours, depending on the emotional mood of the person. For example, when you are in a state of calm, then you will exude a white Aura. When you are in a state of anger, then you will exude a red Aura. Sometimes Auras may also be a combination of different colours. There is technology now that can show the colour and strength of someone's Aura. I have had mine checked. One day, it was light in colour and extended far beyond my body. This didn't surprise me as I feel I live in a state of calm, clear energy and my inner emotional landscape is positive. If you were to have an opportunity to get yours checked today what do you think the results would be? Strong and white? Or weak and maybe red? Maybe you feel like it may not show up at all.

This is what I want to teach you. This is my mission right now: To help you understand that you can empower yourself and create a strong, positive Aura that will not only affect your overall sense of well-being. It will affect your relationships, your business, and your life as a whole.

YOUR HUMAN SYSTEM

Through my own exploration, I began seeing and noticing a pattern in how my Aura was being affected by different things in my life. As I continued to study this in myself, it became clear to me that that there were specific things in play, and it was all rooted in my mind. Having a strong background in technology, I began to clearly see how our own minds behave like supercomputers. (Stay with me here!) Just like a super computer, we have our own operating system and the ability to run many programs at once. We are constantly juggling responsibilities, taking in the world around us, assessing how we feel, and determining what we need. The list could go on and on! Just take a moment right now: close your eyes and connect to all the "programs" open in your mind that are constantly running. Relate that to being connected to your own unique operating system of your mind. Now imagine that a computer virus was implanted into one of your programs and began affecting your thoughts. Computer viruses are designed to spread to all parts of a computer with the goal of eventually changing the computer, more often than not, making it completely dysfunctional. This is what can happen in your mind. A negative thought may enter your mind about something specific. Maybe a co-worker engages you in conversation about a rumour that someone is up for raise (one that you applied for) or on your coffee break the barista makes a mistake on your order and you feel it ruins your morning. I call these viruses of our thoughts Human Errors. In its most basic form, Human Errors can be outlined as the following emotions, or what I like to call Thought Bugs:

- Anger
- Suspicion
- Craving
- Comparison
- Low self-esteem
- Procrastination
- Getting stuck in negative thoughts

What it can be boiled down to is that these negative thought bugs can enter into your mind, which in turn creates negative energy. This leads to stress and a weakening of your Aura.

I'm sure you can think of a definitive moment, probably even within the last day or the last week, where you can see how your own errors were affecting your core system and negatively impacting the energy around you.

Luckily, we have a set of more positive emotions and various ways of reacting that counter the negative ones. I have identified these and aptly named them our Human Features.

Primary Human features that combat the errors include:

- Love and kindness
- Acceptance
- Forgiveness
- Courageousness
- Patience
- Authenticity
- Gratefulness

One can think of these features as a built-in tool box to combat negativity. This is always at our disposal! I want to help you identify where these positive emotions are in you, so that you may have access them and strengthen the energy that you are putting out into the world and your Aura.

Look, I am not a psychologist. I am not a therapist. I am, however, a believer in how we show up to our work and interact with those around us will have a deep impact on the life we are creating for ourselves. I have firsthand experience. I have taken myself from a place of negativity and darkness to a place of possibility. I have watched my newfound passions and work flourish, along with my relationships, personal and otherwise.

This is a different way of looking at things. This just isn't your usual "Be positive" message. This is connecting into the fact that as humans, we have a distinct design in place to help us truly create a good life for ourselves. The foundation of this is to truly feel happy and positive from the inside out, so that what we engage with is affected by our positive energy. Think of the last time you had an encounter with someone who you felt emitted a positive or happy energy? How did it make you feel? How did you react? You truly have the power to combat these negative thought processes (bugs) already in you! Don't you want to be the one truly living in your potential and sharing your positivity with everyone and everything in your life?

THE "AWESOME LIFE" IS WAITING FOR YOU!

Let's get down to business. Thanks for sticking with me. If you have continued reading to this point, then I want to applaud you! It means that you are deeply interested in living your best life.

Side effects of a mind free from negative Thought Bugs may include:
- General feelings of happiness and relaxation
- Genuine connections when meeting people
- A mind free from clutter
- A deep appreciation for the world and people around you
- High levels of productivity
- Willingness to learn new skills
- Gaining more contacts and connections with ease
- Feeling an authentic excitement for projects and self-development
- Being ready to rock your life!

These are just a few of the feelings available to you if you commit to removing negative Thought Bugs from your life, thus strengthening your energy and Aura from the inside out. I wouldn't be here today if I didn't do the work and experience the benefits of being on the other side of the process.

BRING LIGHT TO YOU

My hope for you is to learn how to identify your negative Thought Bugs and stop their process of multiplication. For you to empower yourself with positivity and strengthen your aura. For you to leave feelings of depletion behind and bring your energy back to 100%. For you to share your positive energy with the world and make it a better place!

Never forget: An Awesome Life is within your reach at all times. I believe it. In fact, I will go so far as to say I know it is. I have taken my own life and made it awesome by taking all I have outlined in my work and applying it to myself. Now it is your turn to turn up the positivity in your life and let your Aura shine!

I encourage you to check out my website, www.happinessmountain.com, to receive a free guide on removing your negative energy. In this guide, you will also be given a sneak peek into the app I am developing. The Happiness Mountain™ app will quickly become your new best friend! I developed the Happiness Mountain™ app to be a way to actually track those negative Thought Bugs and coach you to clear your worries and boost your energy levels! By giving you this important tool at your fingertips, I know you will be able to strengthen your energy and basically start living a more happy life! If you haven't guessed already, I love technology and its possibilities for enhancing our lives. I can't wait for you to be one of the first people to try this app and reap its benefits right away at www.happinessmountain.com/app.

BRINGING LIGHT TO YOU SO THAT YOU MAY BRING LIGHT TO THE WORLD

Now that I have given you some insight on how you can truly change your life by changing your own energy, I want to share the ways that Happiness Mountain™ can help you begin to apply these concepts. The process of understanding, application, and execution is key when committing to changing the way your mind functions and, over time, changing your aura.

Now that you know you have the power to change your life via your thoughts, I wonder why you wouldn't want to act now to change your life. Your own personal idea of an awesome life is within reach! I left behind an old way of living and being in order to start on a new path. I am confident that you have the power to do that for yourself as well. We all just need a little help. To be honest, I wish I had connected with these deeper levels of understanding regarding my thoughts and how they affect my life earlier. However, as we all know, timing is everything, especially when it comes to your advancement on both a personal level and a business one. Take this as a sign that it may be time for you to dive into these deep changes. The techniques, once you really begin to understand them, are quite straightforward. I know that you live a busy life and are striving to do your best. However, it takes commitment to change. Why not start now?

Happiness Mountain™ can offer you many tools to get started and help you dive deeper. The first step is easy! I encourage you to head over to my website www.happinessmountain.com to sign up and stay connected to the developments in my work. You will automatically receive an easy to follow guide on how to remove your negative energy, which will be delivered right to your inbox! You will also be given an automatic sneak peek into my app.

THE HAPPINESS MOUNTAIN™ APP

I am constantly inspired by how we connect online through different platforms and technologies. I believe that this can be the start to a great change in how we grow and develop. I designed the app as a convenient way for you to connect to your energy boosting practices on the go. We all spend some time on our phones scrolling and engaging on different platforms. Why not invest that time mindfully instead of mindlessly? The Happiness Mountain™ app, www.happinessmountain.com/app, helps you do that by having the tools you can utilize to boost your own positive energy available at any time!

Features include the following:

- Troubleshooting what is worrying you and replacing that worry with positivity

- Ways to resolve disputes without creating negative energy and affecting your Aura

- Aura boosting activities you can do on daily basis, while tracking your progress with your own private point system

- An emergency toolkit for handling sudden negative situations

- An easy guide to all the Thought Bugs and how to handle them available at a touch of your screen, so that you may continue to learn how you can change your thoughts to more positive ones and keep your positive energy high!

HAPPINESS MOUNTAIN™ FOR KIDS

Calling all parents and anyone who takes care of children! This work isn't just applicable to more mature minds and bodies. It can start when we are young! I am in the process of finishing development on a series of books for children that will cover all the core concepts of my work and Happiness Mountain™, so that we may share these valuable tools and concepts even with the developing minds of the next generation. Of course, there will be interactive games for children as well, because as we all know that some of the best learning happens when we are having fun! This goes for adults too, don't you think? Stay in the loop by connecting with me at www.happinessmountain.com.

MY NEXT BOOK

I am ready to dive deeper and share with you even more in my new book, *Happiness Mountain™: Double Your Happiness, Awesomeness and Spirituality*. In the book we are going to explore deeper than ever before. *Happiness Mountain™* will go more in depth on how you can harness the three levels of energy (Positive/Negative, Aura and Universal) to change your perspective and unlock your perfect life. I want to share with you the techniques and deep processes that will affect all aspects of your life. Remember those 'Negative Thought Bugs' I was talking about earlier? In my new book I will teach you not only how to eliminate them, I want to teach you how to protect yourself from future encounters with 'Negative Thought Bugs' therefore truly creating change in your life for the better. You will also learn techniques on how to recharge your energy, boost your aura and use your new skills for resolving conflicts and affecting your business.

I want you to harness the power of your personal Positive & Aura energies, learn to dance with the Universal energy that is always at your disposable and be able to live at a level of existence that falls in line with your ideal, perfect life. Take a look at the *Happiness Mountain™* diagram on the next page. You can define your perfect life as living with a high level of inner peace, the level of inner happiness. Your Awesome Life and Spiritual Life revolves around being of service to others and helping others. You can live a combination of all levels of the *Happiness Mountain™*. Whatever you personally define as perfection is where you have the power.

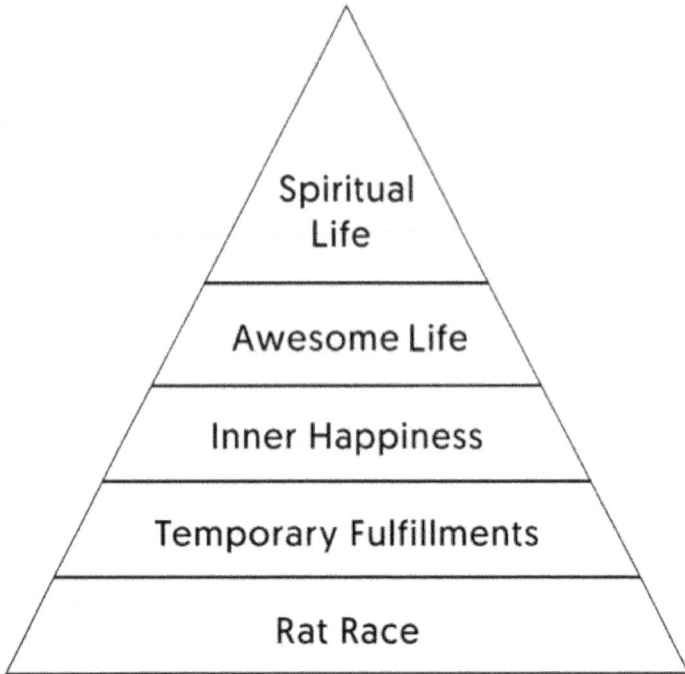

Happiness Mountain™ created by Amal Indi

Some might argue you cannot have a perfect life. I say you already have a perfect life and it is blocked by negative energy from coming into full fruition. This negative energy can be existing as a low self-esteem bug or a comparison bug. You may define perfect life as comparing to others. You may try to achieve things with craving energy. Please remember: You are already whole, complete and perfect. You cannot access your full power because of the negative energy being generated by your thoughts. When you learn to remove those negative thoughts as I teach you in *Happiness Mountain™*, you will realize how much power you have in life. This will be your turning point to harness the energy to power-up your personal, business and spiritual life! In the book I will give you all the tools and techniques to accomplish that. After reading my new book *Happiness Mountain™* you will be able to shift your life to a new paradigm that is not only accessible but exciting. How do you think it will feel to lead a perfect life? Can you think of even one thing that may change for the better if you decided to investigate how you could crush your negative energies, enhance your positive energies and essentially eliminate future worries from your life? ... Wow! I am excited for you just thinking about it myself! I know the profound changes it created for me in my life and I look forward to hearing how it affects yours.

YOU CAN LEAD AN AWESOME LIFE

My hope for you is to learn how to identify your negative Thought Bugs and stop their process of multiplication. For you to empower yourself with positivity and strengthen your aura. For you to leave feelings of depletion behind and bring your energy back to 100%. For you to share your positive energy with the world and make it a better place!

Never forget: The Awesome Life is within your reach at all times. I believe it. In fact, I will go as so far to say I know it is. I have taken my own life and made it perfect in my eyes by taking all I have outlined in my work and applying it to myself. Again, your negative thoughts may say your life is not perfect, which might include your low self-esteem, cravings, or comparison bugs blocking you. Don't let these bugs create negative energy. Instead, clear them and power-up the personal, business, or spiritual aspects of your life. Never forget you have the power over your own mind- NOT your negative Thought Bugs. Now it is time to power-up the positivity in your life and let your Aura shine!

I encourage you to check out my website, www.happinessmountain.com, for the opportunity to stay connected to the global community of people who have already begun to use this work to boost their positivity and create their

Awesome Life in their personal, business, and spiritual domains. I can't wait for you to begin using The Happiness Mountain™ App to start training your energy to stay positive and even get stronger. Of course, I encourage you to visit www.happinessmountain.com to stay connected and be in the know as to what is coming down the pipeline with this life changing work.

I have dedicated my life to bringing these concepts and work to you. I know you can change your energy and begin to not only affect your own life, but the entire world. I believe deeply that when as many people as possible align their energy to a higher, more positive state, then we can truly make a collective difference. Let's start today!

Amal Indi lives in Vancouver, Canada, and is the founder and CEO of Happiness Mountain™ Inc. After 20 years of working in technology and corporate banking, Amal is on a mission to give people the possibility to live with their full potential in their personal, business, and spiritual domains. He has found innovative techniques and tools to remove negative energy and power up your personal life, business life, and spiritual life. Ultimately, you can make the world a more awesome place for everyone. He believes that technology has the potential to transform the minds and energy of people and facilitate change. Amal wants to help people around the globe live a positive and enriching life through the energy-based tools and techniques of this innovative system he has developed to strengthen your energy and help you live a life full of happiness and potential. Find his story and work at www.happinessmountain.com.

Purpose and Living Your Passion Cure

RON BELL

T his chapter is about Ron Bell's defining your *Purpose and living your Passion Cure*. It offers 10 powerful ways to discover true inner peace and happiness. However, in order to understand each step in this process, we need to begin with two basic definitions.

First we'll look at the word purpose. Purpose is the reason for which something is done or created or for which something exists. Some useful synonyms are motive, motivation, cause, occasion, reason, basis, justification. When used as a verb, purpose is one's intention or objective. It has such synonyms as: intend, mean, aim, plan, design, decide, resolve, determine, propose, aspire. For example, I know someone who gets up every morning and purposefully begins to work on his goals at 6 am. He does not stop until 4 pm. He has a plan, the resolve to fulfill it and the motivation to meet all challenges. In other words, while his day is filled with purpose he also has a purpose.

Next we'll define the word passion. Passion is strong and barely a controllable emotion. The man in the previous example works, plays and rests on purpose. He is driven. The emotions he feels are strong, sometimes barely controllable; he needs to move through his days with a sense of purpose, resolve and determination. He is filled with passion.

The first question that begs to be asked, of course, is how do you get to such a place? How do you get on purpose and become motivated to stay there? One step is to begin with an inventory of your strengths. The way to do this is to ask yourself a series of questions. Ask yourself a question and the mind will always answer. Always. For example: Are you loyal? Do you pursue your assignments with pertinacity? Why do you act the way you do when faced with difficulty? Are you courageous? Honest? What are your greatest assets? Write your answers down on a piece of blank paper. Do you act on purpose throughout the day? How about passion—do you act with and feel great emotion that drives you forward toward your purpose, a passion that takes your strengths and carries them toward perfection? Create a list of the resources you, as an individual, possess and that you can get behind both mentally and emotionally.

There's wisdom in knowing your strengths: Men or women who know their strengths are never without resources. They can turn to this tool box whenever some difficulty or trouble passes through their lives. Your strengths can be the difference between staying on task (or purpose) and falling back into the rut that most people live in. This is why it's so important to combine purpose and passion. Acting on purpose from minute to minute depends completely on your motivation, and your motivation is very much about passion. The greater your emotional investment in your action, the greater will be that which drives you. Think of passion as the gas that runs the car of purpose. You can't go anywhere on an empty tank. Similarly, you can't run on gas tainted by water. You will eventually falter and stall, placing you right back where you used to be. Yes, purpose and passion go hand in hand.

Now for the *10 powerful ways to discover true inner peace and happiness:*

STEP 1: EMBRACE CHANGE

Did you know that the average person hates change? In fact, they spend their lives trying to build cocoons to keep change at bay. Little do they know that, like the butterfly, we are a chrysalis that is turned into a human version of the butterfly by the pressure of change. If, in your life, you are receiving the same results, you must change what you are doing. Then and only then will you receive a different result. Knowing this, shouldn't we learn to embrace change? Get serious about it! Determine what your natural gifts and talents are. This list will be different than the one you made regarding your strengths. This list is about the thing(s) you know, without a doubt, that you are better at than anyone else. In fact it's probably the one single and natural thing you dream about spending your life doing. (Your true Passion).

How do you begin working on using the strengths and talents you've found to create positive changes in your life? The answer is, become conscious of the choices you make on a moment-to-moment basis. Create awareness of what it is you are thinking, saying and doing throughout your day. Then begin to make these choices on purpose and with passion.

Part of making positive change in your life is identifying your dreams. Your dreams will probably rotate around those gifts or talents you discovered a few steps back. For example, somewhere within that dream vacation is also a dream of how you came to be there. What is your dream job? Why? How can you achieve it? I'll tell you how ….

Once you've clearly identified your dreams, you need to understand that turning them into reality is all about goal setting. It requires that you reverse engineer those big dreams, breaking them down until you arrive at some task you can do today and in the days to come.

Stay disciplined and focused. Once you begin setting daily goals it's very important that you stay disciplined. No weekdays off or early check-outs for you. True goal-setting requires that you spend your day focused on each goal you apply yourself to—one at a time, hour by hour and day by day—until you reach that far away dream which can create and inner peace and true happiness.

STEP 2. FIND PURPOSE AND PASSION

Self-empowerment is the actuation of the self through minute-to-minute choices. These are choices made on purpose, with real focus and passion. It's the result of knowing your strength and your dreams and having a plan, through goal-setting, to use those strengths to get there.

However, all these changes can increase your stress levels. Happily, the way to decrease stress is to take the task at the top of your prioritized list of goals and put all your focus on it, never thinking of any of the other tasks on your list until you have finished the one you are currently working on—even if you don't finish your list of daily goals. In such a case they just get added to the next day's list. Why does this work? It works because it eliminates worry (most likely one of your biggest stressors). It will also let you get more done than any other system you might happen to try.

I'll tell you a secret. The system of goal-setting I've been talking about will create a new zest for life in you, and it will leave you happier. Why? You'll have virtually eliminated worry in your life. Secondly, our minds are goal-oriented machines. By creating a focused plan, you'll be tapping into that problem-solving aspect of your mind, and it will leave you satisfied at the end of each day. A person who is satisfied with where they are in life and with whatever they have will generally be happier.

Lifestyle change, which is huge and what most individuals desire, will come as you change the decisions you make throughout the day. Make the conscious choice to make positive decisions leading to your goals. Make an extra sale a week, 50 more telephone calls per week, or take on more responsibility at work—all these changes tend to lead to lifestyle changes. So can your daily decisions: the choice to not go for a coffee break at the local café puts more money in your pocket every day; the simple choice to smile in the moment can bring all sorts of changes to your life as you meet new people and enamour the ones you know. The list is endless. Change your moment-to-moment choices and watch your life alter before your eyes.

As you become a more confident decision-maker and an even more stellar goal-setter, you'll undoubtedly notice that your personal confidence will grow exponentially. There's something about making the right choices and doing the right things (for you) that boosts people's confidence immensely.

And … you may never work again. This point may seem silly to you, but it holds a kernel of truth. When you begin to act on purpose, pursuing goals designed to bring you your greatest dreams, you'll find that you're no longer working but rather you're having fun and experiencing happiness. You'll be filled with a passion for action. No longer will problems plague you, because you'll know that each problem solved takes you a step closer to the fulfilment of your daily goals and your ultimate dreams.

STEP 3. SEVERAL INTERTWINED METHODS FOR OBTAINING INNER PEACE

One way to obtain inner peace is to go in deep with meditation. There are many different forms of meditation, and it's beyond the scope of this piece to point you in a specific direction. Suffice it to say that meditation serves two purposes: 1) to clear the mind and 2) to create an intense feeling of focus and well-being. By going deep into a meditative state you can face whatever it is that lies before you with a renewed sense of passion and clarity of thought. Sounds good doesn't it?

Joining up and networking with individuals who are on a "passion" quest for the gift or talent that will light a fire beneath them like never before is heady stuff and very important. You must surround yourself with "like" minded individuals. These are people who are excited by the prospect of finally discovering and doing what they were born to do. They're a special club of people who are passionately working on achieving their dreams. And that excitement will rub off on you. I am personally involved with a Success Training Company called PEAK POTENTIALS. If you would personally like to take your life to the next level, I recommend you attend their self-development seminar. It's a true life-changing event. You may register at: http://lifepurposeandpassionbook.com/ -- a great group of people to rub shoulders with! You've got to know this will lead to greater inner peace.

Fasting is a biblical way to truly humble yourself in the sight of God (Psalm 35:13; Ezra 8:21). King David said, "I humble myself through fasting." Fasting can transform your prayer life into a richer and more personal experience. Fasting can also result in a dynamic personal revival in your own life and can make you a channel of revival to others.[1] It most definitely leads to inner peace.

And finally, self-reflection, like fasting, can clear your mind. Serious thought about one's character, actions, and motives can bring a sense of cohesiveness that can't help but create a greater sense of peace.

STEP 4. DISCOVER YOUR LIFE PURPOSE

Many people never discover their "life purpose." They get caught up in earning a living, raising a family and a thousand other different things. They might play wistfully with a hobby they love or they might daydream about doing something they secretly think would bring them the true contentment they desire. But they never quite reach the point where they make the jump to living their dreams.

The truth of the matter is that *Success is ... taking action.* One must become actively aware of what it is that they were put on this earth to do. You know what this is. It's that secret dream you hardly dare to dream of. Or it's something people have always said you were born to do. Whatever your gift or talent is, deep down you know it. You just need to bring it to the forefront of your mind, you need to seek true awareness. Next comes action. The average person never takes enough small steps to create the momentum needed to move forward into the life of their dreams. Success is ... taking action. Break your dreams down into ever smaller tasks until you reach the point where you have a list of things you can do now—today. Act on them. Take the thousand baby steps that will add up to massive action. Begin right now. The number of people who begin the journey to their dreams but never get there are countless. It's not their fault. They never knew that they had to carefully analyze their actions. A ship gets to its destination by making the minute-to-minute analysis of its position and then making course adjustments necessary to stay moving in the direction of the targeted port of call. Do not try to "eat" the whole elephant. Focus and take small steps to reach the bigger goal. Take realistic steps to reach your goals and obtain your dreams because, when you make unrealistic goals, you set yourself up for frustration and ultimately failure. People must chase their dreams in the same way. We must constantly adjust what we do to make sure we stay on the right path.

You might think this path will be too stressful. And stress can kill. Everyone knows that. Well, if you don't want stress then you must first accept that happiness, joy, contentment and beauty are the natural order of things. Did you know that 47% of all cancer cases is due to "pent up anger and resentment? Strive for continued happiness. It may be a stretch at first, because I can almost guarantee you don't have these things in your daily life. It's not your fault. Chances are no one ever taught you how to consciously focus on bringing them into your daily life. That's right: the key to removing stress from your life is to purposely bring happiness, joy, contentment and beauty into your life by making the right choices on a minute-to-minute basis. It's that simple and that difficult. But you can do it. I know you can.

You really must choose the environments mentioned above. Toxic environments kill everything in their path. You must choose to live differently, every minute of your life. And you can't expect to be valued if you don't, first, value yourself. Change your thinking and your actions will change, and people will sense it. They will look at you differently. Because we are, most definitely what we think. The Process of Manifestation is: Thoughts lead to Feelings. Feelings lead to Actions. Actions lead to Results. Let's get Positive RESULTS in our lives!! Your inner thoughts will determine your outer world!

STEP 5. LEARN TO THINK POSITIVELY

Many people think that positive thinking implies seeing the world through rose-colored lenses, and ignoring or glossing over the negative aspects of life. You know—the glass is half full instead of half empty. However, positive thinking actually means approaching life's challenges with a positive outlook. It does not necessarily mean avoiding or ignoring the bad things; instead, it involves making the most of potentially bad situations, trying to see the best in other people, and viewing yourself and your abilities in a positive light. Such habits reduce stress and increase your level of contentment and happiness.

Why is positive thinking contagious? This is what I call a "no brainer." Who would you rather hang out with: the guy who is always the life of the party or the grumpy guy in the next cubicle at work? The choice is obvious, right? But why is it obvious? It's obvious because the guy who's the life of the party makes you feel good—about the party and about yourself. And therein lies the key. If you alter how you view yourself and your abilities, other people will alter their behaviours regarding you. Call it the psychology of the masses or some other technical term: it doesn't change the fact that, in general, people respond to us based on how we see ourselves.

How can you turn negative thinking into positive thinking? Positive thinking must be made a habit for it to work. That means you must be willing to consciously choose your thoughts or your response to what is going on in your life from a minute-to-minute standpoint, until the process becomes second nature. This takes commitment and hard work, something most people aren't going to do for a process they don't even understand. But you now understand, don't you?

An example of positive thinking: "The history of the baby frog.......

Once upon a time there was a bunch of baby frogs....
… participating in a competition. The target was to get to the top of a high tower. A crowd of people had gathered to observe the race and encourage the participants.....

The start shot rang out.......
Quite honestly:
None of the onlookers believed that the baby frogs could actually accomplish getting to the top of the tower.
They said things like:"Åh, it's too difficult!!!
They'll never reach the top."
or: "Not a chance... the tower is too high!"
One by one some of the baby frogs fell off…
...Except those who quickly climbed higher and higher..
The crowd kept on yelling:
"It's too difficult. Nobody is going to make it!"More baby frogs became tired and gave up...
...But one kept going higher and higher.....
He was not giving up!

At the end everybody had given up, except the one determined to reach the top! All the other participants naturally wanted to know how he had managed to do what none of the others had been able to do!

One competitor asked the winner, what was his secret?

The truth was.......

The winner was deaf!!!!

The lesson to be learned:

Don't ever listen to people who are negative and pessimistic...

...they will deprive you of your loveliest dreams and wishes you carry in your heart! Always be aware of the power of words, as everything you hear and read will interfere with your actions!

Therefore:

Always stay...

POSITIVE!

And most of all:

Turn a deaf ear when people tell you that you cannot achieve your dreams!

Always believe:

You can make it! Stay Positive!!!

STEP 6. ELIMINATE NEGATIVITY

Until you've become strong enough to be able to ward off the negativity in situations it would be a great idea to avoid watching the news. It might even be good to avoid television altogether. Why? Because there's so much that is negative or that will counter your attempts to live a contented and happy lifestyle that it could severely hamper your efforts.

Just to make a point. I turned on the television last night when I got home, and set about having a relaxing evening. There were at least six channels that were talking about current terrorism threats and many other channels were carrying shows full of violence and bloodshed. Tell me how that works to help you change your mindset in a positive way? I'm not saying not to watch television, but be very careful what you put into your psyche.

What was said previously goes double for negative environments. If a situation truly is negative, how do you expect to truthfully change your thoughts about it? You can do it, but you'll most likely be kidding yourself. The way to stay positive, contented and happy is to make certain your day is filled with light and beauty, not darkness and ugliness. Make sense?

Adopt healthy eating habits. Is thinking about having a hamburger and French fries for lunch really bad thinking? It is if you're overweight and your goal is to lose that weight. To adopt healthy eating habits (and this goes for anyone, not just the overweight), one must make those moment-to-moment positive choices we've been talking about. The choice to choose a salad over a hamburger and fries is simple—if you are acting on "purpose."

Focus on the "whats" not the "what ifs." What can I do about my current situation to make it a positive and joyful experience? What if this wasn't happening to me? What if I just skipped out? What if I made the effort to enjoy myself? Which of these questions will make certain my thoughts and actions are going to ensure the best possible experience? If you chose question the first one, then you're beginning to get the hang of "positive thinking." Do not look at opportunities and situations in life and say, "I'll believe it when I see it". You will miss opportunities over and over again. It's the exact opposite, YOU WILL SEE IT WHEN YOU BELIEVE IT" Have Faith! Just because you do not see the seeds growing, doesn't mean, they are not growing. Please refer to the story of the Chinese Bamboo Tree—the story of patience.

What do you love? What do you love to do? I'm not just talking about work here. What leisure activities do you love? What can you do to make sure you build as many of these activities into your days as possible? Remember the goal-setting process? By placing leisure activities on your priority list, you'll be sure to do them when their turn arrives. If I've booked a tee time at my favourite golf course for 2 pm, then I know my workday is going to end at two, and I can prioritize my daily to-do list accordingly, knowing that no matter what happens I will quit working at that time.

Will such practices work every time? Of course not. Life is full of problems and obstacles. But I can guarantee that such habits will bring more pleasure and inner peace into your life than any other method I know of.

STEP 7. DEVELOP YOUR "SELF"

The threat to your continued self-development is inaction. Regardless of the reason or excuse, you can't change anything about your life unless you take purposeful, massive action. Those countless moment-to-moment choices that lead to action of unimaginable proportions must be made on purpose and with specific results in mind. Failure to do this consistently is the one major threat to the achievement of anything you want—include self-development. Best Selling Author T. Harv Eker was quoted saying, "Rich Minded People continue to learn and Grow and Poor "minded" and Middle Class people think that they already know." It's key to invest in your continuous self-development.

Find a life coach. Why do you need a life coach? A person who has already done the things you want to do can guide you past the many pitfalls that lie before you. She can also ensure that you make the right moment-to-moment decisions. She's been there, remember? A successful life coach can shorten your journey by years. Isn't that worth the investment of money and effort? I think it is.

Associate with like minds. People have the ability to affect others through changes in their mindset and their actions. Imagine what could happen if like-minded people came together. The effect could be explosive. I know for a fact that two like-minded people can increase their success exponentially. It's like they form a third mind, a "mastermind," that lifts them up and carries them forward. The effect increases as you add more people to your group. You can even have more than one mastermind group. Some will focus on personal development, some on work and some on investing. You can have a mastermind group for just about any aspect of your life. Anytime two or more like-minded people get together great things can happen.

Read self-help books. Again, you can benefit from those who have gone before you. There are thousands of self-help books out there. And they cover just about any subject you can imagine. Invest in them. There isn't any rule that says your mentor must be a live person. Books can and do teach people how to attain their goals in life.

Enrol in self-development programs. Dale Carnegie, perhaps the greatest motivator ever, taught many, many thousands of people how to achieve their dreams. His books touched many others. His speaking courses were genius in motion. Enrolling in similar courses can give each of us the spark to move forward, to take action with a purpose. You don't have to do this thing alone. Find a program to help you along.

Everything that has been laid down in this outline could be considered the process by which you can change your character and/or your abilities for the better. Don't you think that such positive changes would make you happier and more at peace with yourself? All that remains is for you to take action.

STEP 8. LEARN THE LAW OF ATTRACTION

The law of attraction is the name given to the term that "like attracts like" and that by focusing on positive or negative thoughts, one can bring about positive or negative results. This belief is based upon the idea that people and their thoughts are both made from "pure energy" and the belief that like energy attracts like energy. One example used by a proponent of the law of attraction is that if a person opened an envelope expecting to see a bill, then the law of attraction would "confirm" those thoughts and contain a bill when opened. A person who decided to instead expect a cheque might, under the same law, find a cheque instead of a bill. Although there are some cases where positive or negative attitudes can produce corresponding results, there is no scientific basis to the law of attraction.

How to use the Law of Attraction and how it may assist you: "The one who speaks most about illness has illness. The one who speaks about prosperity has prosperity," Esther and Jerry Hicks write. "You attract all of it." By focusing on something, you make it happen. And oh how true this is. In life focus can be everything. Think about something long enough and hard enough and you're sure to become attuned to actions that can make it happen. The intense focus will also increase the chances that you will act on your thoughts when the opportunity presents itself.

It's very easy for people who know this secret to believe that like attracts like, but I caution against that belief. What is actually happening is you are becoming more alert to and more ready to take the actions that will lead to whatever it is you want. Make enough such choices and you are almost certain to arrive at your destination. And it can really feel like magic!

Successful people know many of the things I've been writing about. They know that if they put themselves out there they will eventually bump into something like they are looking for, whether that's a person, a place, or a thing. It's all about focus and the choices that result.

The old adages are that we reap what we sow, that what goes around comes around and that what we give so shall we receive. The whole point is that our focus/choice combination works every way. Put your focus on giving something different to your community or to your family and you will tend to make choices that will reflect that change in thinking. The changes will be noticed by others, who you can be certain will eventually return the favour however they can. It's a great way to live and you can reap rewards beyond your imagination.

STEP 9. TAKE YOUR QUALITY OF LIFE TO THE NEXT LEVEL

There is nothing so strong and so life-affirming as love. Felice Leonardo "Leo" Buscaglia PhD (March 31, 1924 – June 12, 1998), also known as "Dr. Love," was an American author and motivational speaker, and a professor in the Department of Special Education at the University of Southern California. He believed that, the more you love, the greater becomes your capacity for love, a rather contrary vision of what love is like. This was a view of love as having the infinite power to change us and those around us. In fact he said as much in the following quote: *Too often we underestimate the power of a touch, a smile, a kind word, a listening ear, an honest compliment, or the smallest act of caring, all of which have the potential to turn life around.* – Leo Buscaglia

I could go a step further and say that the greatest phenomenon in the universe is the concept of love. Many see God as love. A fact I know is that the more you give love, the more you tend to receive, whether you're thinking of God or yourself or another. Yes, self-love is important. We can only love our God or our spouse or anyone else as much as we love ourselves. How can it be any different? We can only give what we have and what we know.

This also goes for the intensity of our love. It is our deep belief and our intensity that gives us the power to affect others. For this reason it is a worthwhile exercise to practice intensity of love.

I also admonish you to give as you hope to receive. We have all heard this platitude. It has lost what power it might ever have had. But this does not diminish the truth. If you are willing to sacrifice to give to another or to your community, then you fundamentally change yourself. You become more willing to help, to put yourself out there. People will remember this. So, when the time comes when you are in need, as we all are at some point in life, you'll find that all your sacrifices will be remembered and returned tenfold. It may not be in the way you expect, but it will happen. There's too much anecdotal evidence to believe otherwise.

And as I close, love once again comes into play. Open your heart to the universe and it will fill you up. Give all this back and you will feel as you have never felt before. Some call it a religious conversion, others refer to it as enlightenment; still others speak of a sense of peace and happiness. The bottom line is that you can't love too much. It's impossible. Love can't be used up, so don't be afraid to reach out (take action) for what is waiting for you. You won't regret it.

STEP 10: MORE WAYS TO FIND TRUE INNER PEACE

Apologize and Forgive – When a person apologizes for a wrong he's done or forgives a wrong done unto her an amazing thing happens. All the negative thoughts and emotions you were harbouring simply melt away. You may want to know why this is the case. The answer is incredibly simple: you change your focus. Your moment-to-moment thoughts and actions turn away from what was bothering you and suddenly things are new again.

Relax – Inner peace is a state created by you. Taking time out of your busy day to just relax and allow your mind to drift away to your favourite destinations is a good place to start.

Be Grateful – Happiness and contentment come from being grateful for what you already have. Take your focus and place it on thoughts and actions that indicate to you that you are, indeed, grateful.

Go Outdoors – Nature is the great healing balm. A walk in the forest, a stroll through your garden, a ride on your bike or any other outside activity that gets your body moving and breathing in fresh air can't help but improve your disposition.

Go Inside Yourself – The best way I know to go inside myself is meditation, which is the practicing of certain techniques that allow you to clear your mind, heighten your focus and then point your mind in the direction you wish to go.

Know When to Stand Firm – Inner peace is sometimes reached by facing down a problem, whether that be an intense short-term task or a longer-term worry. Face down your problems, find the best way to deal with them, do those things and then forget about them. Inner peace will be yours.

Learn the Power of Surrender – When people talk about surrendering they're usually talking about God. There's something amazingly powerful about giving up yourself and your problems to the holy spirit. I think the largest part of this is that you are giving up all your worries. Joe Tye (CEO and Head Coach of Values Coach Inc., which provides consulting, training and coaching on values-based life and leadership skills.) once said "Worry is ingratitude to God in advance." Think about that for a moment!

Be the Love You Want to Feel – If you want to feel loved, then you must not only love yourself but demonstrate your love for others. It's a risky thing to do—putting yourself out there like that—but you already know that we reap what we sow.

Be of Service – Strange things (good things) happen when you give of yourself to your community, the first of these being a sense of belonging, which goes a long way to creating inner peace.

Be Here Now – And, finally, making the choice to be in the moment, to enjoy each and every one we have during our time on earth, creates such a sense of joy that one soon relaxes and finds a sense of inner peace. Try it, you'll see.

How To Gain Abundant Wealth

KAY EVE

This advice is aimed at two groups of people – first, those who heard the name of God but have not taken further action and second, those from a practising Christian background who have lapsed.

If, however, you are an atheist then the teachings described here cannot help you. I wish it were otherwise, but I cannot change how the universe is. Without belief, you cannot have God's spiritual help in your search for wealth and wellbeing. Without belief, you must rely on only human knowledge to see you through the difficult times.

The issue is that Christian teachings are haunted by two very wrong ideas. Firstly, the notion that suffering is good for you and that we must each "bear our own cross". One such example is that Mother Theresa of Calcutta refused medicine to patients in her "hospitals" because of the belief that suffering was "good for the soul." This was not the Middle Ages, but only 20 years ago, showing how deeply embedded the idea that "suffering is good, yet pleasure is dangerous" still is within Christianity even to this day. I won't deal with this idea here extensively other than to say that there are many churches that will tell you the good news, that God wants us to be happy – and what's wrong with being happy? I advise you to visit an evangelical church. The worst that can happen is you'll have a good laugh.

The second wrong impression within Christianity is that it is wrong to long for material gains. Jesus famously overturned money changers' tables in the Temple. He said "it is easier for a camel to go through the eye of a needle than for someone who is rich to enter the kingdom of God". I hope to show that what God hates isn't making money, but acquiring it dishonestly or hoarding it all to yourself. Instead, Christian teaching encourages us to live a comfortable life with your loved ones and to do good with the excess. This interpretation is often ridiculed as "praying for money", particularly by spiritual people who I want to reach. Good people also deserve to succeed! So I ask you to keep an open mind, and to give me benefit of a doubt and give careful consideration to what I have to say.

I'm certainly not saying that the Bible tells you that if you ask for gifts from God then they will just fall into your lap! Many of the good things that Gods gives us are quite unasked for – sometimes things will just come miraculously. However, what the teachings say is that if you ask, He will help you to help yourself. You will have to supply the hard work for financial success or personal happiness, but God will be right by your side.

Read on and discover God's love for us all. I know in my heart that if we start looking closely, we can find messages of encouragement that God gives mankind, messages that have mostly been covered over or shunned. I'm here to try and bring out the truth, that God wants us to know His desire for everyone to be happy and have a meaningful, fulfilling life.

And so, I thank God every day for everything that was created directly by Him and indirectly by humans in our world. I am so grateful to be here amongst all of you today.

THE GREAT DISCOVERY

When we think of our galaxy, we know that it is shaped just like a fried egg with the yellow yolk in the middle and a disc of white surrounding it. In the outer edge of the disc is our sun, with one of its planets that we call Earth, which is found to be a safe place for all living things.

During the 19th and 20th centuries, scientists gradually discovered how the universe and the earth formed and evolved. The human race had already been running around planet earth for thousands of years, living and breeding on the planet quite successfully when at peace but killing each other in times of war. Those ancient people had no knowledge of how the earth was formed, but still some of them knew the wealth teachings, and so they came to be wealthy and successful.

If you look at the world's religions today, the only faiths that teach us how to live with Abundant Wealth are the teaching of the Torah for Jews and the Old and New Testaments for Christians. The Abundant Wealth teachings were recorded in all the books we call the Bible, within which one can acquire the keys to unlock wealth and happiness.

More and more people are now searching for words of guidance from the sages of old and from modern businessmen and businesswomen alike. One may not realise that the roots of the valuable teaching from modern day "coaches" actually originate from Christian doctrine. Most people in our modern world do not know how to use and apply the keys successfully to their own lives. But through keeping in mind these teachings and keys, it is possible to achieve your goals and attain wealth, success, happiness and wellbeing.

The only thing that can maintain an abundance of wealth, success and prosperity is God. He has played the biggest part in all our lives whether we realise it or not. People can say they don't believe in God, but if they do, they won't have access to His teachings for success. A lot of people believe in other religions, but abundance only comes down to us from the most powerful, the most almighty, the most gracious and the most merciful one called God. The truth is that there is only one key in the universe and God himself has the key. By praising and asking God for His Abundant Wealth's codes you will learn how to apply the codes for yourself and become successful in every aspect of your life.

The simple question is how to become wealthy? If you believe in God, you will discover these Abundant Wealth's codes and be able to use these codes to unlock for yourself whatever your heart desires, in your personal life, business, work or family. When you have learned this, you will have learned the secret of one of the most satisfying experiences of life. You may say "Well, that's okay for those who already know God, but what about people that do not know or have never heard of God before?"

If you happen to be later, that is ok; it is very easy to join this group of enlightened. By way of illustration, I will call it a club. As you already know, if you aren't a member of a certain club, you cannot receive the access, knowledge or privileges which members can. To be in God's presence is like being in God's club just like the other Christian or religious sects' clubs.

With God we have free will to choose to worship Him or not. That is your personal choice. God does not need anything from you except to receive your sincere love and your worship. God does not want you to sacrifice anything to

Him. He has already sacrificed his own beloved son Jesus Christ for us over two thousand years ago.

Firstly, you need to believe that there is such a thing as the Supreme Being who is commonly referred to as "God", with His own special holy names by which He would prefer to be called. Without this belief, you will not have your wealth key's codes to work. If you do not believe that God exists, then why in the universe or on earth would you expect any of His Abundant Wealth's codes to work for you?

Secondly, endeavour to believe that God has the power to grant you your Wealth codes to unlock the doors of the universe and give you all aspects of success and abundant wealth. God can indeed be reached directly, for there is no distance between Him and His Son.

If you are not in God's club you are an outsider, you will not receive full wisdom to understand all of God's instructions laid out before your eyes. As Jesus has told his disciples in Mark's Gospel,

Mark 4:12 Jesus said, *"When they see what I do, they will learn nothing. When they hear what I say, they will not understand. Otherwise, they will turn to me and be forgiven."*

The "forgiven" word here means to be freed from wrong decisions, wrong choices, etc. So your faith in Jesus will make these mysterious passages, the codes, clear.

EVERYTHING IS POSSIBLE

First you need to do everything physically and mentally possible to make a good connection with God!

When we discover that we are known and understood by God, it can be a very profound and moving experience. Sometimes your spouse or best friend may know or understand you on the surface, but deep down you may feel like you are alone. And yet no matter how well you are known or understood by others, no one can understand you better than God himself. As King David has put it;

Psalm 139:1-4 NIV

"O Lord, you have searched me and you know me. You know when I sit and when I rise; you perceive my thoughts from afar. You discern my going out and my lying down; you are familiar with all my ways. Before a word is on my tongue; you know it completely. O Lord."

If you believe that God exists in the world like the ancient people of past times did, then you will want to worship the Almighty for the successes in your life. But how can you actually get a real and intimate connection to Him? The sincerity of your heart is the key to success.

Three steps to Calmness:

1. Find solitude with God, away from other people and distractions. By shutting out the sights and sounds around, you will make it easy to tune in with God.

2. Find a comfortable position, select a chair or a corner of your bed. Go to the same place at the same time in the same position every day. Consistency is of the utmost importance.

3. Before you begin, relax and take a few deep breaths. Let your mind be quiet and your body relaxed. When your mind quietens, you may know the conscious presence of God that says "Be still and know that I am God." Psalm 46:10

Now you are ready to start making a connection.

Three Steps to Listening:

1. The first step of prayer is to praise God, such as by citing the Lord's Prayer as in Matthew 6: 9-13. Let your prayer begin by praising God and you will soon find yourself in a frame of mind with Him.

2. Let some positive thinking and praying enter your mind. The secret of success is thinking and believing positively, and the same is true in prayer.

3. Ask Him to speak to you and tell Him about the things that matter to you. Whatever problems or difficulties you have, you can rely on Him for comfort, stability and the material things that the world has to offer. Once you have things off your chest, remain quite still and relaxed and listen!

By modern standards in the developed world, very few of us are really suffering. The atheists down the street will probably have all they need and live physically as well as you, perhaps even a little better. Yet, if you ask God, you will receive more blessings than they ever will and be in a better place with a better quality of life, with all the things you ask for that can be truly beneficial to you.

EXPECTING THE UNEXPECTED

Secondly you must believe that he has the power to help us and wants to help us all!

When you have asked God for the things I have described above, one final step remains - the "receiving in advance", or the assurance that your prayer will be answered. You need to thank Him and to strongly assert your confidence that He is going to provide the answer to your request. Filling your heart with positive thoughts will help to ensure that God will allow these things to happen.

Yet, how can you be assured that a constant relationship with God will produce answered prayer? The answer lies within the Abundant Wealth codes, within the heart of answered prayer, and within the following everyday Bible verses, such as;

Matthew 17:20
If you have faith as a grain of mustard seed, you shall say unto this mountain, "Remove from here" and it will move. Nothing will be impossible for you." (The "mountain" in this parable of Jesus means one of our life's great crises.)

Matthew 21:22
If you believe, you will receive whatever you ask for in prayer.

Mark 21:24
Therefore, I tell you whatever you ask for in prayer, believe that you have received it and it will be yours.

However, do not mix up the word "Faith" with "Belief". To believe that God can answer and is able to deliver all of the things being asked for in prayer, this is not faith. Everyone can have faith. The prayer of faith means trusting in God to do something but truly believing in God means to know that God is honest and will do what He says He will. It is to believe unhesitatingly that He is on the verge of doing it and that even now, the answer is on the way to you.

Many people also misconceive faith as desire, but this is false. Many people want success, but longing, wanting and desiring success is not faith. Desire, rightly directed, can produce faith and may lead you to faith, but in itself it is not faith. When you have known God intimately, you may experience a genuine re-dedication of your heart, only to be disappointed that your prayer went unanswered. This is because God may judge that the "good" thing was not what you really need at that time. He will give you something else that's good, something that benefits your life.

Faith is a common commodity. Everyone has faith. Atheists have faith that there is no God. Animals and pets have faith in their masters. Children have faith in their parents and we have faith in our Governments to watch over our nation. It is only faith in God through truly believing in Him that will reward you with your heart's desire. As James says in James 1:6-8;.

"But when you ask God, you must believe and not doubt, because he who doubts (unbelief) is like a wave of the sea, blown and tossed by the wind. That man should not think he will receive anything from the Lord, he is a double-minded man, unstable in all he does."

Believing is an act of total trust in God; it doesn't require information, knowledge or certainty – only the free and joyful surrender in His goodness. To help with this, look for the "invisible" gifts of God. They are clearly seen in the many good things that have already happened, things that are usually taken for granted. However, God alone will not change the course of some worldly events. For instance, He doesn't interfere with situations in which people have created chaos around themselves. They must deal with the consequences of their own actions. God is very constant, but for victims caught in the chaos He will turn things around for those who have the absolute trust in Him.

Each code of Abundant Wealth is laid out in the Bible for anyone to read. It has rarely been used before because few pay attention or even try to find out the meaning that God has given freely to everyone. Established religions tell people that praying for money or success is the sin of "avarice", yet churches get rich while their congregations are told to be content with what they have. But who can build a hospital or invent a new medicine without money? It is not the money that is inherently bad; it is the people that do bad things with or for it.

Most modern day sages who have written books about God's wealth codes have hidden the source of these gifts, saying that they come from the universe instead of from God Himself. One can ask for wealth, success, love and happiness until your tongue hangs out, but you will not receive the answer without asking only God himself.

Asking others who pretend to be God for favours will end in disastrous results for you, even if it may appear to be beneficial at first. Many rich and famous people have made deals with others but there is a steep price that must be paid for this false hope. Through Jesus Christ, we have paid already and there is nothing to fear when asking for success, as long as it is done without wickedness or dishonesty.

If you are still skeptical about the wealth key's code then it will not work for you. I wish you good health and happiness, but if you remain doubtful you might as well throw this book away! To have everything that you need and desire you must make a total surrender of your heart, your love and your belief to God, the powerful and the almighty who has created this world and the universe. As is said in Hebrews 11:1-6;

"Now faith is being sure of what we hope for and certain of what we do not see .... By faith we understand that the universe was formed at God's command, so that what is seen was not made out of what was visible .... And without faith it is impossible to please God, because anyone who comes to him must believe that he exists and that he rewards (Abundant Wealth to) those who earnestly seek him."

THE TRUTH REVEALED

Who is "God" and what's wrong with the idea of a general "Supreme Being"?

God defines Himself as the great lover of mankind, and many Bible verses reveal the depth of this love.

Jeremiah 9:24

"I am the Lord, I show unfailing love, I do justice and right upon the earth; for on this I have set my heart"

Jeremiah 31:3

"I have loved you with an everlasting love; I have drawn you with loving kindness."

Mark 11:29-33

"A new command I give you: Love one another. As I have loved you, so you must love one another."

Most religious texts, Hebrew and Muslim alike, give many names of God in their own Language - seventy-two in Hebrew and up to ninety-nine for Muslims. The only one that God told Moses directly is found in Exodus 33:19. "I will call out my name, Yahweh" ("The Lord"). Even so, there are many other names given to God which reflect the compassion, kindness and generosity He had for different peoples, such as;

Yahweh-Jireh Lord will provide

Yahweh-Rohi Lord is my shepherd

Yahweh-El Shadia   Lord Almighty

Yahweh-Shalom   Lord of peace

Yahweh-Rapha   Lord of healing

Yahweh-El-Olam   Lord everlasting

Yahweh-M'kaddesh   Lord who sanctifies

As mentioned in the Old Testament, no one can see God face-to-face and live to tell, due to his vast and glorious power being too much for our bodies of mere flesh and bone. For this reason, when God appeared to Moses He covered Moses' body with the shadow of His hand.

Exodus 33:19

"I will make all my goodness pass by before you. For I will show mercy to anyone I choose, and I will show compassion to anyone I choose."

Exodus 33:20

"but you may not look directly at my face, for no one may see me and live."

As we know from the Bible, God created the universe, the world and all living things on it. Among these creations was the Sun, which produced the light and heat that God commanded to shine upon the Earth as God had wanted from the beginning.

Genesis 1:1 & 31

"In the beginning God created the heavens and earth...And God said "let there be light."

And so, humans were born on Earth in multitudes, and from them God selected the nation of Israel and the Jewish people to work with Him. Much of the Old Testament tells of God's love towards this nation. Yet men were disobedient and uncaring towards God, turning away to worship frightful and false gods instead. And so the New Testament tells us that God sent his son, Jesus Christ, to be born as a human among us and so that we would love and worship him again. As the Bible says, if we accept that Jesus is our Lord and the son of God, then we become God's adopted children and have the right to call him Father and to ask for his Wealth Keys.

Matthew 7:11

Jesus says, "Ask and it will be given to you; seek and you will find; knock and the door will be opened to you......which of you, if your children ask for bread, will give them a stone......if you, then, though you are evil, know how to give good gifts to your children, how much more will your Father in heaven give good gifts to those who ask Him."

So what do we know about God so far? We know we can ask Him for help in all matter of things and that nothing is too big or small for Him to handle. We can ask Him for guidance in all of our problems because He truly cares, and we can also ask him for whatever we desire and it shall be done for us. If we know God intimately and are not happy with our present situation, then we can always ask Him to change it for the better. We must remember that there is no god other than Yahweh-God who proved his love for us by laying down his own son's life for our benefit. The people who get their prayers answered are just simple people like you and I. We must never doubt in Him and we must always rest assured; God is real. He was, He is and He will be in everyone's life.

THE ASKING

But how can you actually go about asking God for Abundant Wealth?

Everything is possible with God for those who love Him. You can trust in God that all that you ask will be fulfilled before you draw your last breath on earth, no matter how long it takes. An example can be seen in Luke Ch. 2 where Simon, the old Jewish prophet who was full of devotion to God, asked that he might meet the Messiah in his own lifetime. God answered his wishes and promised Simon would meet him before he died.

Luke 2:27-29

Led by the spirit, Simon went into the Temple. So when Mary and Joseph came to present the baby Jesus to The Lord as the law required. Simon took the baby Jesus into his arms and praised God, saying "Master, now you are dismissing your servant in peace according to your promise."

It is God's will that his children will possess Abundant Wealth and all that they desire. And so we now need to concentrate on how to build a relationship with God in order to receive his true blessings. Like any relationship, one has to dedicate oneself to make it happen. Though it is common knowledge that true human relationships are not always easy to maintain, it is different with God for he loved you first. He longed for you to love Him back, and it is up to you now to do your part.

There are only a minority of people who have a true belief in God's love and will see a miracle happen to them in their lives. It is hard for most people to love and believe in God, especially being surrounded by modern technology where things must be seen, heard, touched, felt or sensed in order to be real. God and belief in Him have become almost a myth, but the key to finding true belief is to discern God's love in your own life, which can be done in Five Steps.

1. Ask God to step into your heart and reveal his truth to you. You can do this anywhere or any time as long as it feel right to you. Once you have accepted God and Jesus into your heart, you will become an adopted child of God and you can begin building the relationship.

Revelation 3:20

Jesus says; "Look! I stand at the door and knock. If you hear my voice and open the door, I will come in, and we will share a meal together as friends."

2. Begin worshiping and praising God, whether out loud or silently in your mind. Concentrate on God's love towards your every being. Ask God to clean not only your heart, but your mind, your soul and your entire being. You must create the purest atmosphere to get positive reception of God's intuition and that small voice that speaks directly into your heart.

Nahum 1:7

"The Lord is good, a refuge in times of trouble. He cares for those who trust in him."

3. Study God's word within the Old and New Testaments, asking God for the wisdom to discern the Bible's lessons. The parables are not easily understood the first time they are read, so you must ask for God's help in deciphering them. Only then may you apply them to your personal and professional life, as generations of God's children have done before you.

Mark 4:9-12

"Anyone with ears to hear should listen and understand" ... *"You are permitted to understand the secret of the Kingdom of God. But I use* parables *for everything I say to outsiders, so that the Scriptures might be fulfilled."*

Understand that things which you ask God for can come quickly or slowly depending on how ready you are to receive them. God knows that if he gives them to you when you are not ready, you will lose these gifts or become unable to cope with it. In time, if we use His words and apply them to our lives, we are sure to receive everything that we need or want and we may continue to ask for more.

4. Have faith that God will deliver. You can see how often many people gave up on asking things from God because they could not see any results

coming out of their prayers. Most people have forgotten what the most important part of the prayer is. They forgot to get the most authoritative person to support and speed their request so that it was heard quickly by God. Much like in a court case where you need a proper barrister to work with you to ensure the judge will rule in your favour, it is the same with God. You need your spiritual brother Jesus Christ to help with your prayers so that the Heavenly Father may execute your request. Always ask God for your needs in Jesus' name. But remember, only God knows when the time is right for you to receive his gifts, much like a doctor who knows when to give treatment to his patient. Once you understand all of the above, you can use the Bible Keys and apply them to your personal life.

Isaiah 55:11
God says; "It is the same as my word. I send it out and it always produces fruit. It will accomplish all I want it to, and it will prosper everywhere I send it."

5. Finally, you must give thanks. After you have given your prayer request, you must thank God with all your heart. The more you thank Him, the quicker his blessings will come to you. You must now concentrate on believing one hundred percent in your heart that your request is now heard by God.

There is a final condition that you need to make it work. You must understand that if you have received God's answer to your request, you will now need to get to work on the request you made. You will not receive any kind of blessing that you have not earned, much like the old wives' tale of "help yourself first and God will help you."

Proverbs 10:4
"Lazy hands make a man poor, but diligent hands bring wealth."

Proverbs 22:29

"Be sure you know the condition of your flocks, give careful attention to your herds."

The above five conditions are absolute must-dos if you want your prayer to be answered and to succeed in having God bless you with wellbeing, happiness and success in your life.

Roman 10:11

"As the Scripture says. Anyone who trusts in Him will never be put to shame."

GRATITUDE

Giving thanks is of vital importance, but just Giving to others is also important!

How well do we know the meaning of the word "gratitude"? If you want Abundant Wealth from God, you must be able to change your attitude and behaviour towards what you have been given already.

1 Timothy 6:17

"….. Their trust should be in God, who richly gives us all we need for our enjoyment. Tell them to use their money to do good. They should be rich in good works and generous to those in need. By doing this they will be storing up their treasure as a good foundation for the future so that they may experience true life."

You already know how to trust in God for the things you have asked for. Now you need to know how to act while you are waiting for God to bestow upon you the things you desire. Even if you do not have much, you still need to appreciate what you do have, that which has sustained you until now. You may hate your menial job or be in a boring business, but you must not condemn it. After all, it has kept you afloat until now.

The Key to this is that now you know how to turn things around. While appreciating what sustained you, from its original roots, God will bless it and turn it into a good thing.

Matthew 25:29

Jesus says; "For everyone who has will be given more, and they will have abundance. Whoever does not have, even what they have will be taken from them."

This first sentence above means that your need to be grateful for all the things you currently possess. This appreciation will make them become more important, even if right now they seem worthless to you. The second sentence does not mean that God will take your things away, only that without your appreciate of them, the few resources you have tend to be squandered.

In the physical realm, you may be in a job that you hate but are desperate to leave. You may want God to answer your prayers and to help you out of this predicament. In this instance, while you wait for God to manifest things that you have prayed for, you must learn to imitate God's spiritual realm in order to turn it into your real world.

Romans 8:24

".... But hope that is seen is no hope at all. Who hopes for what he already has? But we hope for what we do not yet have, we wait for it patiently."

If you know the mind of Jesus Christ, you will know that when He was in human form, everything was beautiful and perfect in God's eyes. Jesus was without worry and he was on Earth solely for the purpose of doing God's work. Nothing could harm or touch him because God's power was within him. When he was laid on the cross of crucifixion, it was because Jesus allowed himself to be, in order to fulfill the scriptures and be sacrificed as a lamb of God for all of us.

Therefore, you must have gratitude for Christ's gift because he paid with his life for your sins. You can be free of anxiety, stress, worry, distress and ill health because Jesus removed all those bad things from you. All hardships are of the physical realm; you can be free of these struggles by switching yourself to the spiritual realm.

When you know that God is by your side, your mind will be sharp and focused. No matter what sort of negative thoughts arise, you must not listen to them. They're trying to lure you away from God and all the good things that he has in store for you.

According to Christian teachings, two cosmic broadcast stations – the Light and the Dark – send signals to our brain. Any thought that is loud and clear, which urges you to react to a situation, without a proper plan, that is the enemy – the Dark. But if the thought is barely audible, if it is a soft voice emanating from the recesses of our mind, it is the song of the Light. If you are greeted with a sudden flash of intuition or inspiration, you can be certain it is from the spiritual realm.

The key to taking control of your life is to ignore the loud noise in your head and to take time to concentrate on the small, quiet sounds from God to guide you. When you succeed in blocking out the negative thoughts that manifest themselves as our greedy and selfish egos, the Light signal and all the good thoughts that come along with it are free to fill our minds. The best ideas can come forth at once and without hindrance, and you can see the way to wisdom.

In the Old Testament, during the time that king Ahab ruled in Israel, Ahab did not worship God. He killed all of God's prophets except one, Elijah. Elijah was afraid and asked for God's help. He went into a cave where he spent the night praying and waiting for God's instruction.

1 Kings 11:13

"Go out and stand before me on the mountain" the Lord told him. And as Elijah stood there, the Lord passed by, and a mighty windstorm hit the mountain. It was such a terrible blast that the rocks were torn loose, but the Lord was not in the wind. After the wind there was an earthquake, but the Lord was not in the earthquake. And after the earthquake there was a fire, but the Lord was not in the fire. And after the fire there was the sound of a gentle whisper. .... And the voice said "What are you (still) doing here, Elijah?"

Thus we can know that the gentle, whispering voice is from God, not the enemy.

You now have all the Abundant Wealth Keys in your hands, and can begin to apply them to all aspects of your life. You can begin to see success in all areas, from your personal and family life, to your professional and business life, and to your community as well.

Finally, remember this. If you care for other human beings like God cares for you, you will continue to receive God's blessing. You will please God if you lend Him a hand, doing charitable work for those less fortunate than you in this world that God has made for us all.

Family Is Everything

DAN ROGERS

Hundreds of years ago wooden ships brought immigrants to the shores of what would become the maritime provinces of Canada. Why did the pioneers brave starvation, malnutrition, disease or shipwreck?

Today, a number of immigrants arrived at Pearson International Airport in Toronto, Ontario. Why did they leave their countries, their jobs and friends to try and carve out a new life in Canada?

Ask such questions of either group and you would likely receive the identical answer: "To build a better life for my family," they would say. Why? Because family is everything!

In 1916 a young couple, Clarence and Lizzy, got married and boarded a train to northwest Saskatchewan. The rules were that if you were over eighteen, married and agreed to live on and work the land, the government would grant you a quarter section, which is 160 acres or 65 hectares.

At first they plowed the virgin fields with a team of oxen. The prairie grass roots were so thick that the girl had to follow along behind the plow, cutting the roots of the prairie grass with a butcher knife. Her first three babies miscarried. Then, on her fourth pregnancy, the boy rounded up just enough money for one train ticket to the closest town that had a hospital (Lloydminster). He took her in a horse drawn wagon across the prairie for many kilometers to the train station, put her on the train and returned home to continue working the fields. The girl gave birth to a healthy baby girl named Grace. That baby girl was my mother.

My grandmother was what was known as a Bernardo child. She was in a program based out of England that was founded by a man named Bernardo. Orphans and children whose parents could not afford to look after them were shipped to Canada to live on farms. Some of the families treated the child as one of their own, while others treated the child as a slave. The end result, however, was that they got to Canada. And it worked, albeit slowly. So ... my mother had a better life than her mother ... I am having a better life than my mother ... and my son, an only child, came home from the hospital not only to his own bedroom, but to one that had a four piece en suite bathroom. Also, by the time my wife and I are gone from this world, he will be an automatic millionaire.

My hope is that you and your family can accomplish this quicker than we did. We were slow learners. It took us over a century to create wealth. But the fact that you are in Canada and reading this book already puts you in the group that is most likely to succeed. Do you find that hard to believe? Then just think of all the people who came home from work today and are either checking Facebook or watching reality TV. They definitely aren't reading a book about how to succeed financially.

THE PURPOSE OF THIS CHAPTER

The purpose of this chapter is to help educate you to use whatever money you have to benefit you and your family in the long run.

The first thing I want to do is ask you a question: What is your biggest asset? Many people will answer that question by stating what they own. Various answers will be the most obvious ones like my house, my car, my life insurance policy, my retirement fund. But the real answer is you or, to be more accurate, it's your ability to earn a living.

Now, consider that the average annual income in Canada is around fifty thousand dollars (at time of printing). That means in a typical forty year career you will have grossed two million dollars. Yet, most Canadians don't own two million dollars of mortgage free real estate or don't have two million dollars in the bank or even in an insurance policy. Why is that?

It's simple mathematics ...

Mr. A and Mr. B both moved to Canada about fifty years ago from the same country. They both got jobs at the same company for the same wage. But Mr. A saved up his money for a down payment on a house and also budgeted in the monthly premium for a permanent life insurance policy, while Mr. B spent much of his disposable income on trips back to his homeland, coffee shops, take- out food, and cigarettes.

Both A and B died about twenty years ago. The daughter of Mr. A inherited a mortgage free house and a life insurance policy, while the son of Mr. B ended up with nothing. Because the child of A immediately had cash in hand, from the insurance money, and she chose to live in the house for free, she was able to invest both the life insurance money and the monthly rent she had previously been paying. Meanwhile, the son of Mr. B had to save for years and years before he could get out of the apartment he was renting, because saving up while paying rent is much more challenging. In the end, however, B descendent was able to buy a house and make some modest investments.

Eventually the heirs of both Mr. A and Mr. B died. The grandchildren of A have inherited multiple real estate properties and investment funds easily worth in excess of a million dollars, while the family of Mr. B ended up with only a few hundred thousand, as the real estate and other investments were purchased later in their parents' lives and didn't have time enough to grow. The property may not have even been mortgage free at the time of Mr. B's death.

So, the third generation of the A family are now millionaires, while the same generation of the B family has enough money for a modest down payment on a nice house.

You want to be Mr or Mrs A. Buy a home early and pay off that mortgage. Protect your ability to earn with the proper insurance policies and invest on an ongoing basis. Read on, I'll show you how to do it. But first a discussion about estate planning

WILL AND POWER OF ATTORNEY

We have been talking about estates. These are passed on to beneficiaries through the vehicle known as the will. But, over the several years that I have been in this profession, I have encountered a rather high percentage of people that do not have their wills done. And you do need one. Not a "do it yourself" will kit that can be purchased online or at a business supply retailer. Generally, the legal system does not consider this type of will to be valid. No, I strongly urge you to have a lawyer draw up your will. A good lawyer. A conscientious lawyer. Here's why ...

An elderly widower sells his house, puts the money in the bank, moves to an apartment, and marries a much younger new wife. His lawyer draws up a will stating that his estate will be divided amongst his wife, his three children and his two favourite charities. The lawyer did not enquire about what type of account the money was in or ask any questions of that nature. When the man died, the executor of the estate found out that the bank had advised the man to name a beneficiary to the account, so the man, not being given a full legal explanation of the ramifications, named his wife as beneficiary. So, on his death, the bank immediately transferred 100% of the funds into the wife's name, and there was no legal recourse to get her to divide up the money according to the will. The will became a useless piece of paper. The three children and the two charities received nothing from the fund. That man was my father.

The lesson to be learned is to never assume that a professional you hire is automatically going to do things in your best interest.

Power of Attorney: There are two types of power of attorney: one for personal care, and one for property. This means that you designate a person to make decisions on your behalf should you reach the point where you can no longer make these decisions yourself. **Personal care** refers to topics such as choosing a personal support worker, a nursing home, treatments, medications, and other things of that nature. **Property** refers to topics such as whether or not to sell the house or rent it out or authorize repairs, and whether to sell the car, or cut the lawn or many other property related items.

In listing a power of attorney, remember that you do not have to have the

151

same person for all areas. You could have a daughter who would be the best for personal care, an eldest son who would make the best executor, and a youngest son who is in real estate who would be the best person for property decisions.

I should also mention **Probate** as it is a complicated and frequently costly procedure wherein you must prove the validity of the will. The general rule is that if there is a beneficiary listed on the account, then probate is not required.

When the funds are in a bank, the money could be in one of several different types of accounts. It could be in a chequing account, a savings account, a TFSA (tax free savings account), an RRSP (registered retirement savings plan), mutual funds, segregated funds, GIC (guaranteed investment certificate), a RIF (retirement income fund), and a number of others. The bank would likely ask you to name a beneficiary on the account. This is done to prevent probate. However, remember the story about my father and learn from it. If there is only one person that you want to give your money to, then that is fine, but if there are multiple people, you must name them all.

PROTECT YOURSELF

In order to open this discussion, we need to go back to the reason everyone comes to Canada in the first place. We all know the answer to that one: to build a better life for your family. At the same time, we need to recall your greatest asset. It's you, and if you go down, everything that you worked for could be lost. So we are going to address a very important issue, income replacement. This is generally broken down into two areas; disability coverage and critical illness coverage.

Disability coverage: Disability insurance is meant to replace part of your income (usually 55%) in case of injury or illness. Now, the first thing to know is that not all disability policies are equal. Some give you the right see your own doctor—some do not. And that makes all the difference. The first group of claimants tends to be entrepreneurs who don't want to be away from their jobs any longer than the insurance company wants them to be. The second group of claimants tends to be more the corporate type, a type that encompasses malingerers—those people who are in no rush to get back to work after an injury or illness—the type that breeds distrust in the insurance companies. Make sure you're in the first group.

Integration of benefits: What this means is that if you signed up for a $2,000/month disability policy and you get hurt, and another organization also agrees to pay you let's say $1,200/month, whether it is another insurance company, Workers Safety Insurance Board, the employer, or whomever, then your insurance company only has to pay you the difference of $800/month. You can find policies that don't have this clause.

Return of Premium: What if you are lucky and never get injured? How would you like to get all your money back when you retire, tax free? Yes, there are disability policies available that have this benefit.

Soft tissue injuries/back injuries/sprains/strains: This is another very important feature. Many disability providers are so concerned about people faking injuries that they won't pay out unless something shows up on an X-ray. You don't want a policy like that. You want a policy that will cover you in all cases of injury or illness.

Injury occurs on or off the job: Many employers who provide a benefit plan to their employees will have disability coverage that only covers on the job accidents. While better than nothing, statistically, the average Canadian is more likely to get hurt in a car accident, at home, or while participating in sports and leisure than actually getting hurt on the job. That' the kind of coverage you want.

No limit on number of claims made: This one is fairly self-explanatory. Make sure your provider does not have a clause where they can terminate your coverage if you make too many claims.

Critical Illness/Hospital Sickness Benefits: Let's imagine that you or your spouse were diagnosed with a terminal illness or a debilitating disease. The ill person might wish to do their "bucket list," go back to visit the homeland, see the Seven Wonders of the World, or take a cruise around the world. But from where would the money come? Cash in RRSPs? Sell the house? Remortgage the house? The problem with doing that is it ruins the whole game plan of coming to Canada to build a better life for your children and your children's children.

This is the reason that critical illness coverage exists in a place that already has state funded health care.

And just like disability coverage, it is possible to get critical illness coverage with a Return of Premium Clause, meaning that if you remain in good health, you get your money back at the end.

LIFE INSURANCE

There are many different types of life insurance. It is vitally important for you to know the differences so that you can pick the type that is the right one for your situation.

Reason for life insurance: Do you have massive debt from a mortgage or business loan that if all goes well you will have paid off before retirement? Or do you want to leave your family a lump sum of money for a particular purpose, regardless of whether you die young or old? These two situations require (differing) insurance products.

The standard formula that the insurance industry uses for determining the amount of coverage is: ten times annual salary plus debt. So if you make the average Canadian income of about $50,000 per year and have a three hundred thousand dollar mortgage, then the calculation would be to have $800,000 in coverage.

Term Insurance: Term insurance would be better understood by the public if it were renamed "temporary insurance." With term insurance you are buying a window of time. If you die in that window of time, the insurance company writes a cheque to your beneficiary. If you die outside that window, they cut no cheque at all.

Permanent insurance: Permanent insurance is frequently known by its official name, whole life insurance. If the reason for buying is that you need some security to pay off your debts if you die young, then term is the way to go, but if you want to leave a lump sum to your family whether you die next year or in sixty years, then you will want a permanent product.

Term to 100: Term to 100 is a rather unique type of life insurance that is sort of a hybrid between term insurance and permanent insurance. As we have already read, the disadvantage of a term policy is that it eventually runs out, but the advantage is lower premiums. The disadvantage of whole life coverage is that the premiums are high, but the advantage is that it lasts forever. What if you could get a policy that never runs out but that has the lower premiums more associated with term insurance? Great, right? That's why many companies don't offer the product. But you can find it, if that is what you want.

No Medical Insurance: No medical insurance is frequently called other names such as final expense insurance, funeral insurance, burial insurance, guaranteed issue insurance, instant issue insurance, and perhaps a few other names. It is frequently advertised by way of television commercials, and mail flyers delivered by the post office. The target client is often a retiree whose term insurance has now expired but who still wants to leave a lump sum when he or she dies. People with health problems who will never qualify for standard application coverage also tend to buy this type of policy.

Universal Life: This is another type of whole life policy. It can be a bit complicated, so I'm going to give a brief explanation of this product here. With a universal life policy, a portion of your premium goes into an investment. Over the years, the idea is for the investment to grow substantially. A universal life policy with a face amount of $100,000 would have an additional investment portion attached to it, so after a few decades the policy might pay out in total $150,000, $200,000 or more. Although this seems like a great idea, low interest rates over the past several years have made many people who hold a universal life policy realize that the projected payout at the end is going to be considerably lower than what the agent had suggested way back when the policy was first taken out.

The moral of this story is to make sure you sit down with a financial professional who will do a "needs analysis."

PLANNING FOR RETIREMENT

RRSP stands for Registered Retirement Savings Plan. An RRSP isn't an investment, it's a shell in which you can store all sorts of different kinds of financial plans and investments.

An RRSP could contain stocks, bonds, mutual funds, segregated funds, Guaranteed Investment Certificates, syndicate mortgages, Guaranteed Investment Accounts, just to name some of the more popular products that a typical Canadian RRSP might contain.

What an RRSP does is let you defer income tax. It is designed for Canadians who know that they are going to be bringing in less money after they retire than they are currently bringing in now. Canada Revenue Agency (CRA) charges income tax on a sliding scale depending on the income of the person. Someone who doesn't earn much income may pay no income tax at all, where someone with a high income might pay out 40% of their pay to income tax.

Life Income Fund: A life income fund generally comes from a company pension. Some employers offer a company matched retirement plan, meaning that whatever you put into it, they will contribute an equal amount. When you leave the company, it is recommended that you do something with it. The reason is that if the company runs into financial trouble, your retirement fund could be gone, or at least reduced. It has happened before, and will most likely happen again. Instead, if you quit, get downsized, or retire, you should move that money out of there and put it with an investment firm. That way, the success of your former employer will have no influence on the fund.

Various investments

Mutual funds are what are known as securities. The agent or broker must hold a license regulated by each provinces securities commission. Mutual funds are really just a collection of various stocks. They were designed for the purpose of the small investor being able to get into the stock market without a large cash outlay and with a lower risk. There are thousands of different funds out there, and virtually all of them are quite heavily diversified. This is both good news and bad news. The good news is that if one or a few of the companies that are inside that particular mutual fund take a huge nose dive, it won't cause your fund to drop too dramatically. The bad news is really the opposite side of the same coin. If a few of the stocks in the fund soar tremendously, your fund won't go up all that much because of all the other stocks in there that remain steadfast or have dropped. Mutual funds have no guarantees whatsoever, so if your fund dropped way down, you have only two choices: you can cash out at a loss, or you can hold onto it for enough years and hope that it rebounds satisfactorily. Mutual funds are also subject to fees known as Management Expense Ratios, or MER. If your fund's MER is 2%, then on a one hundred thousand dollar investment, expect to pay two thousand dollars per year in fees.

Segregated funds are very similar in concept to mutual funds. Segregated funds are sold by life insurance companies. Many financial experts describe segregated funds as "mutual funds with an insurance policy wrapper". Segregated funds must be kept separate from the insurance company's regular finances, hence the name. A "seg" fund and a mutual fund may both be investing in the same stocks, the main difference between the two, is there is a guarantee with a seg fund. The guarantee in a seg fund is generally either 75% or 100% of the original investment, depending on which plan you take. That means that you are guaranteed to get back either 75% or 100% of your money, even if the fund loses money. You will have to hold onto the fund for an agreed upon length of time, usually ten years to get this guarantee. And it is important to know that this guarantee is not free. A seg fund will have extra fees associated with it to cover this guarantee. If you cash out before the agreed upon time, you get what is in the fund, whether it has gained money or lost money, less any fees. If the seg fund rises in value, most plans will allow you to "reset" the guaranteed amount to this higher amount, however, that would mean that doing this will reset the amount of time, usually ten years, that you must hold the fund.

Depending on which plan you take, 75% or 100%, if you die while the funds are down, your beneficiary will receive 75% or 100% of the fund.

Guaranteed Investment Certificate (GIC): A GIC is a savings account where the interest rate is pre-set. There is an amount of time, generally two years, three years, four years, or five years that you must keep the money in the account in order to obtain that interest rate. If you withdraw the funds earlier than that date, you won't get the agreed upon interest rate. The longer you keep the money locked up, the higher the interest rate you can get.

Guaranteed Investment Account (GIA): The simplest way to describe a GIA is that it is like a GIC, except it is carried by insurance companies, just like seg funds, and the guarantee activates in the event of the contract holder's death.

If the contract holder dies while having a GIA, the company guarantees the highest of the two following things: either the balance of the account on the date of death; or 100% of the sum invested in this account.

Syndicated Mortgages: A developer who wants to build a condo tower, a commercial office building, or any other large construction project can generally only get conventional bank financing up to a certain percentage of the cost of the project. The remainder of the amount he needs has to come from someplace else. When you agree to give the developer your money, you go on title, the same way that your bank is on title for your house, if you have a mortgage. Syndicated mortgages have been around for a long time, but ordinary folk like you and me have only started hearing about them in the past few years. The reason is that they used to be reserved for those with very large sums to invest, like a million dollars. It was only relatively recently that the industry opened up the market dramatically by lowering the minimum investment to twenty five thousand dollars. Generally, the syndicate mortgages that have come across my desk pay 8% per annum, simple interest. It is important to know the difference between simple interest and compound interest. With compound interest, you receive interest on your interest, but with simple interest you do not. A typical syndicate mortgage locks your money away for a period of time, frequently three or four years.

Gold and other precious metals: The only reason that I am even mentioning this topic is because I am told that there are people on the radio urging us to buy gold. On the financial security pyramid or pillars, or ladder, or however you would like to refer to it, precious metals are to be considered at the top, right up there with collecting works of art. This means that it is something that would be recommended to do after your house is mortgage free, and you have amassed considerable wealth and assets.

REAL ESTATE

Buy vs Rent: There are always those who debate whether or not it is better to rent and invest more in the market, or buy real estate, and subsequently have less money left over at the end of the month to invest. Remember that home ownership has two entirely separate goals. The first one is to make money on it, either by buying low and selling high, or by making improvements to the property, thus increasing its value, or by paying off the mortgage so that you no longer have the expense of making payments. The second goal is to improve your quality of life. You have your very own residence without being at the mercy of a landlord, should they decide to sell the property, or raise the rent, or move into it themselves, or move a relative into it. You also have total control over what colour you would like the walls painted, the types of light fixtures, window coverings, faucets, countertops, and a host of other features.

Buying Real Estate: The first thing you will require is the **minimum down payment**. When you buy with less than twenty percent down, this is what the banks refer to as a high ratio mortgage. This requires you to have mortgage default insurance. The most popular organization the banks use to obtain mortgage default insurance is the Canada Mortgage and Housing Corporation (CMHC), a crown corporation. Two other companies that offer this are Genworth Financial Canada, and Canada Guaranty. They will charge a fee, and blend it into your payment. This can only be avoided by having a minimum of twenty percent of the purchase price of the property already saved up and available. For a first time home buyer, this could be difficult. Most of the property purchases I have made had CMHC on them. I still found this to be the lesser of the evils when compared to paying rent.

Next, you will need to **obtain approval for the mortgage**. You should do this before looking at any properties. There are two ways of doing this. The first is to talk to your own bank branch. The second is to use a mortgage broker. The advantage of using a mortgage broker is twofold. First, they do all the work, don't charge you and get paid a referral fee from the financial institution where the mortgage is placed. The second advantage is that they will frequently work with multiple lenders, giving them and you more choices. One thing they will be looking for is your Total Debt Service Ratio (TDSR). This means that all your payments, mortgage, utilities, and other things such as car loan payments and line of credit payments should not exceed approximately forty percent of your overall gross household income. So first of all, you should not be considering real estate if you owe any money on anything else, and yes, that includes your car.

The next thing is your need to have established a **credit rating**. There are two credit rating services. The most popular one is Equifax, and the other one is TransUnion. You can obtain your credit score from these institutions yourself at no charge. They will probably try to get you to pay for it, and they will quite likely offer you the information instantly if you pay, but you can wait and get it the slow way without having to pay. If you are new to the country, or young, or both, you may not have established a credit rating. The first thing is to have a credit card. Obviously, the intended goal is to pay the balance off every statement, thus avoiding any interest payments. If you think you can get by in this world without a credit card, you thought wrong. Not only is it vital in establishing a credit rating, but without one, it is generally quite difficult to purchase anything online, obtain tickets for a major event, rent a car, book a flight, stay in a hotel, and a host of various other situations that will cross your path from time to time.

Types of properties: There are really only four: condo, townhouse, semi, and detached

Condo is short for condominium. You will usually see them in the form of high rise buildings, but there are townhouse condos and even detached condos. With a condo you only own the inside, the condo corporation owns the outside. I'm using simple terminology here. You pay a monthly fee to them and they are responsible for exterior things like the roof, landscaping, snow removal, elevators, and really everything this is not inside your unit.

The next type of property on the scale is the **townhouse**. They can be condos or freehold. If it is a townhouse condo, you pay a fee to the condo corporation, just like a high rise, and they look after the same things like the roof, snow removal, and grass cutting. If it is a freehold, you own the whole thing, and you are responsible for everything. The main items to think about with a townhouse is that you share your walls with someone else.

Next on the list is the **semi-detached**. This has all the same possible downsides as a townhouse, but you are only sharing one wall. The key to a good semi is to have a great neighbour on the other side of the wall. But of course, you have very little way of finding that out until you are already moved in.

A **detached house**, meaning that it is not connected to any other building (you can walk all the way around all four sides), is the ultimate goal, in my humble opinion. In many regions, especially in the Greater Toronto Area (GTA), the detached house is sought after not only for the buffer zone between neighbours, but because many of these houses are ideally suited to having a separate basement apartment with a separate entrance, frequently a side door. This is an excellent way to bring in extra money to offset the high mortgage payment.

GOVERNMENT RETIREMENT BENEFITS

There are five main areas about which you will need to know: Canada Pension Plan (CPP), Canada Pension Plan Survivor Benefit, Canada Pension Plan Death Benefit, Old Age Security (OAS) and Guaranteed Income Supplement (GIS).

The Canada Pension Plan (CPP) is something that you would have paid into during the course of your working career. You can apply for it as early as age sixty or as late as age seventy. If you apply for it at age sixty, you will, however, receive a 36% reduction in benefits. If you apply for it at age seventy, you will get an increase of 42%.

According to the government of Canada statistics as of the year 2015, the average CPP monthly benefit is $619 and the maximum is $1,065.

Old Age Security: The Old Age Security (OAS) is a benefit for which you can apply at age sixty five, as of now, however, there are plans to increase the age at which you can apply to age sixty seven. Time will tell if the federal government sticks to the plan of age sixty seven, or if successive governments decide to roll it back to age sixty five. At time of publishing, the OAS is around $565 per month, however, it is indexed to inflation, so it generally goes up a few dollars per month every year.

CPP Survivor Benefit: If you are the first to die in a spousal or common-law relationship, the surviving spouse should apply for this benefit. It is generally 60% of the deceased partner's monthly CPP benefit, or if death occurs before age sixty five, then this benefit is calculated on the amount that it would have been if death had occurred at age sixty five.

CPP Death Benefit: Only a very few countries offer this benefit. To be eligible for your estate to receive this benefit you must have made contributions to CPP in the lesser of: one third of the calendar years in your CPP contributory period, but no less than three calendar years; or ten calendar years.

The amount of the death benefit depends on how much and for how long the deceased contributed to the CPP. The maximum benefit is $2,500. According to the latest statistics, the average benefit is around $2,300. The CPP death benefit is calculated as the amount equal to six months' worth of your monthly CPP benefit.

Guaranteed Income Supplement (GIS): If you live in Canada and have a low income, this monthly non-taxable benefit can be added to your Old Age Security (OAS) pension, if your annual income (or in case of a couple, your combined income) is less than the maximum annual income. The Canadian government calculates this maximum annual income amount based on numerous different criteria such as if you are single, widowed, or divorced, or if you have a spouse that receives the full OAS pension, or if your spouse does not receive the OAS, or if your spouse is already receiving the GIS and the OAS. You can always go the government's website yourself when you need this information: www.servicecanada.gc.ca

FINAL ARRANGEMENTS

This section will be dealing with an area that most people are not particularly thrilled about discussing. Furthermore, most people are not willing to walk into a funeral home and ask questions. Fortunately, I worked in the industry for ten years, so I'm in the position to not only help you spare your family a lot of grief and hardship, but at the same time, save you money as well.

There are two ways to pre-arrange your funeral: One way is to pre-arrange but not pre-pay. The other, and more preferred way, is to pre-arrange and pre-pay.

Cremation verses Burial: The main reason that 90 % of the people I have talked to about funerals over the years choose cremation, is so they can avoid the cemetery completely.

If you choose cremation, there are five options open to you regarding the disposition of the remains.

1. Your family can take the urn home with them and put it on the shelf. (This is not for everyone, some like the idea, some hate it.)

2. You can have the ashes scattered. Note: this choice is completely legal.

3. If you have an immediate family member that is already in a cemetery plot, most cemetery boards will allow you to place your urn in your

family member's plot, generally for a fee of a few hundred dollars.

4. You can purchase your very own plot and have your urn buried there.

5. Cemeteries have structures called columbariums, or wall niches, that you can purchase for the purpose of having your urn placed there permanently.

Funeral Service Choices: For the sake of simplicity, there are really only three.

1. **A Direct Disposition.** All this means is that you are hiring the services of a licensed funeral director to send a transfer vehicle to your place of death, whether that is a hospital, a nursing home, or your own home. They will pick up the remains and transport them back to the preparation room at the funeral home, arrange for the cremation and return the ashes to you.

2. **A Memorial Service** contains everything a direct disposition contains, but the funeral establishment puts on a service, either in their own building, or in the church of your choice. Sometimes people want it to be held in a different location, such as a club that has their own facilities. It is important to note that with a memorial service, the body is not present, no casket is present, cremation has already taken place, and most often, the urn is present in lieu of a casket.

3. **A Traditional Service**: This is the type of arrangement where the casket is present. I'm not sure why, but many people are under the misconception that a traditional service is not available with cremation. The facts are that there are only two real differences between a traditional service with cremation to follow, and a traditional service with burial to follow. The first difference is that with burial, there is a funeral

procession from the funeral home or church to the cemetery, and with cremation to follow, there is not, because the body has to be transported to the crematorium. The second difference is that with burial, a casket is purchased, and the casket is buried. But with cremation, the funeral home usually provides the use of the casket for the visitation and service, and hidden inside the casket underneath the white satin lining, where no one can see, is the combustible, rigid, leak-proof container that is always necessary with cremation.

"I'm donating my body to science!"

This is what you need to know with regards to whole body donation. Medical schools, or schools of anatomy will accept body donations to train future medical professionals. It is completely different than donating organs. The body must be in very good condition and there must be a need for the body. It is important to remember that if you have a pre-paid funeral and you are accepted by a medical school, the pre-paid funeral fund will be returned to the family with interest.

SUMMARY

What do all of these things I've been talking about have in common? The greatest point of all that I've written here is that there are many ways for you to achieve wealth and grow it. An early mortgage and long-term investments can result in a free home for your loved ones to live in, money for them to live on and funds to grow even more money. They can even take the money they used to pay rent with and purchase yet more investments, so that when the third generation matures, there is a literal fortune waiting for them to inherit.

We also discussed investment vehicles such as real estate, mutual funds and term deposits, touching on various types of each, the idea being to make you aware of the choices you have moving forward. We even talked about how to protect your earning potential with disability insurance and life insurance. The chapter ended with a looked at funeral planning.

You came to Canada to make a better life for your family. This chapter can set you on the proper path to achieve what you wish. Good luck in all you do!

www.ingramcontent.com/pod-product-compliance
Lightning Source LLC
Chambersburg PA
CBHW060559200326
41521CB00007B/614